THE BOOKS OF
JOEL, OBADIAH
JONAH, NAHUM
HABAKKUK AND
ZEPHANIAH

COMMENTARY BY

JOHN D. W. WATTS

Professor of Old Testament
Serampore College, West Bengal, India

CAMBRIDGE UNIVERSITY PRESS

CAMBRIDGE

LONDON · NEW YORK · MELBOURNE

Published by the Syndics of the Cambridge University Press
The Pitt Building, Trumpington Street, Cambridge CB2 1RP
Bentley House, 200 Euston Road, London NW1 2DB
32 East 57th Street, New York, NY 10022, USA
296 Beaconsfield Parade, Middle Park, Melbourne 3206, Australia

Library of Congress Catalogue Card Number: 74-80355

hard covers ISBN: 0 521 20505 0
paperback ISBN: 0 521 09870 X

First published 1975

Printed in Great Britain
at the University Printing House, Cambridge
(Euan Phillips, University Printer)

Please renew/return this item by the last date shown.

So that your telephone call is charged at local rate, please call the numbers as set out below:

	From Area codes 01923 or 0208:	From the rest of Herts:
Renewals:	01923 471373	01438 737373
Enquiries:	01923 471333	01438 737333
Minicom:	01923 471599	01438 737599

L32b

GENERAL EDITORS' PREFACE

The aim of this series is to provide the text of the New English Bible closely linked to a commentary in which the results of modern scholarship are made available to the general reader. Teachers and young people have been especially kept in mind. The commentators have been asked to assume no specialized theological knowledge, and no knowledge of Greek and Hebrew. Bare references to other literature and multiple references to other parts of the Bible have been avoided. Actual quotations have been given as often as possible.

The completion of the New Testament part of the series in 1967 provides a basis upon which the production of the much larger Old Testament and Apocrypha series can be undertaken. The welcome accorded to the series has been an encouragement to the editors to follow the same general pattern, and an attempt has been made to take account of criticisms which have been offered. One necessary change is the inclusion of the translators' footnotes since in the Old Testament these are more extensive, and essential for the understanding of the text.

Within the severe limits imposed by the size and scope of the series, each commentator will attempt to set out the main findings of recent biblical scholarship and to describe the historical background to the text. The main theological issues will also be critically discussed.

Much attention has been given to the form of the volumes. The aim is to produce books each of which will be read consecutively from first to last page. The introductory material leads naturally into the text, which itself leads into the alternating sections of the commentary.

The series is accompanied by three volumes of a more general character. *Understanding the Old Testament* sets out to provide the larger historical and archaeological background, to say something about the life and thought of the people of the Old Testament, and to answer the question 'Why should we study the Old Testament?'. *The Making of the Old Testament* is concerned with the formation of the books of the Old Testament and Apocrypha in the context of the ancient near eastern world, and with the ways in which these books have come down to us in the life of the Jewish and Christian communities. *Old Testament Illustrations* contains maps, diagrams and photographs with an explanatory text. These three volumes are designed to provide material helpful to the understanding of the individual books and their commentaries, but they are also prepared so as to be of use quite independently.

P. R. A.
A. R. C. L.
J. W. P.

CONTENTS

MAP

THE FOOTNOTES TO THE
N.E.B. TEXT

The footnotes to the N.E.B. text are designed to help the reader either to understand particular points of detail – the meaning of a name, the presence of a play upon words – or to give information about the actual text. Where the Hebrew text appears to be erroneous, or there is doubt about its precise meaning, it may be necessary to turn to manuscripts which offer a different wording, or to ancient translations of the text which may suggest a better reading, or to offer a new explanation based upon conjecture. In such cases, the footnotes supply very briefly an indication of the evidence, and whether the solution proposed is one that is regarded as possible or as probable. Various abbreviations are used in the footnotes:

(1) Some abbreviations are simply terms used in explaining a point: *ch(s).*, chapter(s); *cp.*, compare; *lit.*, literally; *mng.*, meaning; *MS(S).*, manuscript(s), i.e. Hebrew manuscript(s), unless otherwise stated; *om.*, omit(s); *or*, indicating an alternative interpretation; *poss.*, possible; *prob.*, probable; *rdg.*, reading; *Vs(s).*, Versions.

(2) Other abbreviations indicate sources of information from which better interpretations or readings may be obtained.

Aq. Aquila, a Greek translator of the Old Testament (perhaps about A.D. 130) characterized by great literalness.

Aram. Aramaic – may refer to the text in this language (used in parts of Ezra and Daniel), or to the meaning of an Aramaic word. Aramaic belongs to the same language family as Hebrew, and is known from about 1000 B.C. over a wide area of the Middle East, including Palestine.

Heb. Hebrew – may refer to the Hebrew text or may indicate the literal meaning of the Hebrew word.

Josephus Flavius Josephus (A.D. 37/8–about 100), author of the *Jewish Antiquities*, a survey of the whole history of his people, directed partly at least to a non-Jewish audience, and of various other works, notably one on the *Jewish War* (that of A.D. 66–73) and a defence of Judaism (*Against Apion*).

Luc. Sept. Lucian's recension of the Septuagint, an important edition made in Antioch in Syria about the end of the third century A.D.

Pesh. Peshitta or Peshitto, the Syriac version of the Old Testament. Syriac is the name given chiefly to a form of Eastern Aramaic used by the Christian community. The translation varies in quality, and is at many points influenced by the Septuagint or the Targums.

Sam. Samaritan Pentateuch – the form of the first five books of the Old Testament as used by the Samaritan community. It is written in Hebrew in a special form of the Old Hebrew script, and preserves an important form of the text, somewhat influenced by Samaritan ideas.

Scroll(s)   Scroll(s), commonly called the Dead Sea Scrolls, found at or near Qumran from 1947 onwards. These important manuscripts shed light on the state of the Hebrew text as it was developing in the last centuries B.C. and the first century A.D.

Sept.   Septuagint (meaning 'seventy'; often abbreviated as the Roman numeral LXX), the name given to the main Greek version of the Old Testament. According to tradition, the Pentateuch was translated in Egypt in the third century B.C. by 70 (or 72) translators, six from each tribe, but the precise nature of its origin and development is not fully known. It was intended to provide Greek-speaking Jews with a convenient translation. Subsequently it came to be much revered by the Christian community.

Symm.   Symmachus, another Greek translator of the Old Testament (beginning of the third century A.D.), who tried to combine literalness with good style. Both Lucian and Jerome viewed his version with favour.

Targ.   Targum, a name given to various Aramaic versions of the Old Testament, produced over a long period and eventually standardized, for the use of Aramaic-speaking Jews.

Theod.   Theodotion, the author of a revision of the Septuagint (probably second century A.D.), very dependent on the Hebrew text.

Vulg.   Vulgate, the most important Latin version of the Old Testament, produced by Jerome about A.D. 400, and the text most used throughout the Middle Ages in western Christianity.

[...]   In the text itself square brackets are used to indicate probably late additions to the Hebrew text.

(Fuller discussion of a number of these points may be found in *The Making of the Old Testament* in this series.)

THE BOOKS OF

JOEL, OBADIAH, JONAH, NAHUM, HABAKKUK AND ZEPHANIAH

✹ ✹ ✹ ✹ ✹ ✹ ✹ ✹ ✹ ✹ ✹ ✹ ✹

THE BOOK OF THE TWELVE PROPHETS

The six books discussed in this volume of the commentary are a part of a larger unit originally copied on one large scroll. It had no special name other than 'the Twelve or Minor (shorter) Prophets', i.e. Hosea to Malachi in the English Bible. With the scrolls of Isaiah, Jeremiah and Ezekiel it belonged to the section of the Hebrew Bible known as 'the Latter Prophets'.

The prophetic oracles, visions, biographies and liturgies – that is, arrangements of prophetic words linked to use in worship – contained in these twelve books were collected over a period of more than 300 years (the middle of the eighth to the middle of the fifth centuries B.C.). The collections were given their final shape not earlier than the middle of the fifth century.

Prophetic literature developed in three stages which partly overlapped. From the first and longest stage came narratives about prophets and their activities. Oracles spoken by these prophets, or believed by their followers to have been spoken by them, were important elements in these stories. These followers were virtually 'schools' inspired by the original prophets and they apparently composed oracles in their prophet's style long after he was dead. This activity went on from the tenth to the middle of the fifth century. Early examples, like stories about Nathan and Ahijah, and later examples, such as the cycles of stories about Elijah and Elisha, are found in the books of Samuel and Kings. The latest form of this kind of literature is found in the skilfully-told story of Jonah, which is, as we shall see, a complete book.

From a second stage came simple collections of prophetic oracles. This stage focused on the interpretation of specific historical events such as the Assyrian invasion which led to the fall of the northern kingdom (Hosea, Amos, Micah, the earliest Isaiah oracles), the Babylonian invasion and the resultant exile (Jeremiah, Ezekiel), and the return from exile (Haggai and Zechariah 1–8).

A third stage grew out of the role of the prophet in worship. With the priests they participated in the great festivals, uttering oracles at appropriate points. Later, prophets' oracles, originally spoken for other reasons, were adapted for use in worship, and the prophet's role became that of fashioning and reciting them. This is seen in the arrangement of the earliest collections of oracles which probably were made under King Hezekiah in the last quarter of the eighth century. Prophecy which belongs within the forms of worship thrived in the seventh century (Zephaniah, Nahum, Habakkuk). Most prophetic literature of the latter half of the sixth century (Isaiah 40–55) and the first half of the fifth century (Isaiah 56–66, Zechariah 9–14, Malachi, Obadiah, Joel) consists of this material. This later form of prophecy often involves preaching – homilies, exhortations, instruction – in which prophetic sayings are expounded to new generations of worshippers. The dating of these later writings is a much-discussed problem.

Apparently the collection of the prophecies of Jeremiah and Ezekiel in the sixth century provided models for the book of Isaiah and the Twelve Prophets in the late fifth century. First come prophecies of judgement, followed by a collection of prophecies against other nations, and concluded by the oracles of blessing and fulfilment. (In the book of Jeremiah, this order is found in the Greek text; in the Hebrew and English, the foreign-nation oracles stand last.) This order fitted the use made of prophetic books in worship by the scattered Jewish communities of that time. Their Bible consisted of the long history of Israel which begins in Deuteronomy and continues through Joshua, Judges, Samuel and Kings and the collected 'words' of the prophets, as the oracles were called. This 'Bible' was soon to be superseded, or enlarged (depending on the viewpoint of the Jewish parties involved), by the formation of the five books of Law (including Deuteronomy). Recognition of the authority of this law unified the two major forces in Judaism: the Jerusalem priests of the rebuilt temple, and the synagogues scattered from Babylon to Egypt to Asia Minor, with their rabbis, or teachers, who played an increasingly large role in the temple at that time. Later the interests of Levites would be represented by Psalms and Chronicles in 'the Writings', the third section of the Jewish Canon, alongside other works such as those of the Wisdom teachers and writers, Proverbs, Job and Ecclesiastes.

Some prophecies were closely related to historical events. Editors noted the names of the prophets and the dates of their activity accordingly. Among the Twelve Prophets, the books of Hosea, Amos and Micah are dated in the eighth century. That century's giants are dealt with in another volume of this commentary. They were primarily prophets of judgement. Haggai and Zechariah 1–8 are dated in the last quarter of the sixth century and are treated with Zechariah 9–14 and Malachi in yet another volume. They are prophets of salvation and hope as was fitting for their time and their place in the scroll of the Twelve.

Of the remaining books in the Twelve Prophets only Zephaniah is dated: the middle of the seventh century. It, like the books which follow, is a prophecy of salvation. The rest have apparently been interspersed in the existing collection of dated prophecies. Joel, like Zephaniah, proclaimed the 'day of the LORD' with both judgement and salvation as phases of the LORD's action. Obadiah, Nahum, Habakkuk and Jonah are various forms of 'foreign prophecy', i.e. against foreign nations, similar to collections of such prophecies in Isaiah, Jeremiah and Ezekiel.

THE UNIFYING SETTING: PROPHECY IN WORSHIP

Although these books were not written by a single prophet, they have a remarkable unity of theme and direction. This is provided by their common relation to what they call 'the day of the LORD'. The theme was apparently a basic motif in the Jerusalem royal festival and its counterpart at Bethel. It is evidenced in Amos' use of the term in the eighth century and continued in the seventh. After the exile the festival was revived and changed to leave out the specifically royal portions.

The zealously anti-monarchist books of Kings provide little information about this royal festival in Zion, but some evidence may be gleaned from the Psalms. Modern interpretations of it vary. One of them suggests that the festival focused attention on the kingdom of the LORD and the rule of David's dynasty in Jerusalem. It probably lasted a week, during which pilgrims from all parts of the realm celebrated in turn: 1. the *LORD's entrance* with a procession following the ark up to the city and into the temple; 2. the *LORD's presence* in Zion, recognizing him as creator and absolute king over the heavens and the earth; 3. the *LORD's judgement* of his partners in covenant, the davidic king and the people of Israel; 4. the *LORD's renewal of covenant* with the king and with Israel which announced again his intention to reign over the nations through his anointed king in Zion.

The unchanging emphasis throughout the period was on the kingdom of God and its manifestation in Zion. Many aspects of classical prophecy, i.e. the prophetic books of the Old Testament, seem to have disappeared from history during the period of reform instituted by Nehemiah and Ezra in the latter half of the fifth century.

In this setting 'the day of the LORD' was the high point of the festival when his appearance brought judgement on the covenant people and the nations. It was the day on which comforting words of grace and election could reconstitute the covenant for a new period. The prophet was God's

4

spokesman for both judgement and salvation. Prophetic liturgies came to be vehicles for the entire 'day of the LORD' setting as well as for the oracles themselves.

The crisis prophets of the eighth century and those of the turn-of-the-seventh to the sixth centuries proclaimed 'the day of the LORD' with overpowering emphasis on God's judgement on Israel. They interpreted the Assyrian and Babylonian conquests in theological and religious terms. The reality of God's judgement, set out in worship, was seen expressed in the historical experiences of the fall of Israel in 721 and of Judah in 587 B.C.

But the main intention of worship relating to 'the day of the LORD' looked beyond judgement on the assembled worshippers. It pictured a salvation accomplished by the LORD's intervention on their behalf as he acted to establish dominion over all the earth.

Joel and Zephaniah are important witnesses to the understanding of 'the day of the LORD' in the Old Testament prophets.

THE FORM AND ROLE OF FOREIGN PROPHECY

The foreign prophecies, or oracles against nations, in each of the larger prophetic books fit into the setting of the royal Zion festival and 'the day of the LORD'. They were means, through liturgy, of defining the LORD's rule over the world. They announced God's action to fashion a situation in which the choosing of Israel could be realized.

Obadiah, Nahum and Habakkuk were liturgical expansions of such foreign prophecies. They were part of the festival's celebration of 'the day of the LORD' with its proclamation of his universal rule.

Jonah was, in a sense, a corrective to a false understanding of foreign prophecies. Too narrow a hearing of their message might imply that Israel was the only nation God cared for, that his being 'for' Israel automatically meant his being 'against' the nations. Amos had protested against such a false belief in Israel's being the chosen people (3: 2; 9: 7). The book of Jonah caricatured the prophet whose only message was one of judgement on the nations.

THE NATURE OF PROPHETIC LITURGIES

The way in which stories about prophets were told stressed the person of the prophet and the setting in which God's word was spoken. This tradition dominated the thinking of those who collected and edited the prophetic books. They introduced the prophets by name, clearly noted the period in which they worked, and sometimes documented the circumstances which surrounded the original spoken oracle. This trend reached its climax in the prophecies of Ezekiel, Haggai, and Zechariah where exact dates were given for each oracle or group of oracles.

Prophetic liturgies were radically different. The person of the speaker or composer was irrelevant. Even the date of origin was not important. They, like the Psalms, belonged to services of worship which were repeated frequently. Origin and authorship were less important than was their setting in worshipful festival.

Yet the principle for the editing of the prophetic books was one which continued to stress the person of the prophet and the date of the prophecy. Editors apparently had no alternative principle to cover liturgical prophecy. Where they were left without sufficient information on date and authorship, they attached prophecies to existing collections, as in Isaiah and Zechariah; or simply grouped them with other prophecies with the sparse information which tradition provided, as in Joel, Nahum, Habakkuk; or used a general title for a name, as in Obadiah and Malachi; or let a story *about* a prophet be listed alongside oracles *by* prophets, as in Jonah.

Liturgies were by nature anonymous. They drew on prophetic materials from antiquity to supplement contemporary compositions. To interpret them one must keep in mind the overall purpose of the ritual within which the prophetic liturgy existed. Yet the liturgies, no less than individual oracles, were historically, socially and religiously relevant to the times and peoples who heard them in worship. They proclaimed a consistent and clear theological message which was well worth hearing again.

THE ROLE OF TEMPLE PROPHETS

The picture of a prophet for most readers is that of a spokesman of protest who attacked established leaders of the temple and of the country as well as prominent practices of religion, such as sacrifice. Vigorous presentations of the work of Amos and others like him have conveyed this impression.

But such a picture is not really adequate to these men, who were not only protesting but recalling their people to what they believed was true belief and understanding of God's will. Nor does it take account of other prophets whose function is to be understood much more within the worship of the temples and particularly that of Jerusalem, which was eventually to stand alone.

The Old Testament tells of prophets functioning at the side of priests in the temples. Their ministries appear to have overlapped. Both groups were organized in guilds to preserve the necessary traditions and to train members for the functions to which they were assigned.

What did the temple prophets do? They sought answers from God for questions about life or occupation which individual worshippers brought to them.

The role of prophets in worship was even more important. Signs of their work are found in prophetic material embedded in liturgical psalms. Prophetic books may also include liturgical material (cp. Hab. 3). In such liturgies visions and oracles are mixed with hymns and prayers to form beautiful and meaningful units. It requires little imagination to see these

7

spoken, dramatized or sung in the temple by prophetic liturgists supported by instruments and choirs. Levitical choirs assumed this place after the exile.

The prophet's role allowed variation in form. Festival occasions and liturgies required new and inspired 'words' for each celebration. In addition oracles of earlier prophecy were drawn from a stock of tradition to be woven into new recitations to accompany dramatic mimes or symbolic acts in festal liturgy.

The prophet took part in worship in smaller circles as well. In these, prayer and the cultivation of prophetic gifts were central. Ezekiel (8: 1) recorded such settings for much of his prophecy.

Prophetic tradition had the resources of writing at its disposal as did other groups in the temple and the city. But prophetic circles were unlikely to have relied on written forms to the extent a modern liturgist would. Much of their tradition showed signs of having been remembered, repeated, and handed down orally.

Temple prophets came under severe attack from several major protest prophets, especially Jeremiah. This does not prove that all temple prophets were false, any more than prophetic judgements on priests mean that all priests were bad. We may judge the temple prophets more fairly if we consider how much of their work was preserved in the Old Testament.

Temple prophets were closely related to liturgical worship and were supplied by prophetic tradition with material for their tasks. Yet they exhibit remarkable individual creativity and originality within the limits afforded them. At times they worked actively for reform and renewal within the organization and liturgy.

THE SEVENTH CENTURY IN JUDAH

The books of Nahum, Habakkuk and Zephaniah are from the seventh century. A brief summary of the history of the period is necessary for clear interpretation.

The century began in the waning years of Hezekiah's reign (726–687 B.C.). He had followed a policy of independently standing up to Assyrian power which cost him a loss of territory and subjected his country to burdensome payments of tribute. But in spite of military and political pressure, which included an extended siege in 701 B.C., Jerusalem and Hezekiah survived. He is portrayed in the Old Testament as a religious reformer, excluding alien religious practice from Judah.

Manasseh (687–642 B.C.) was his successor. He reversed his father's relation to Assyria. His policy was one of total submission to the empire, which was at the height of its power. Assyria even dominated Egypt during the first half of the period. Asshurbanipal, the Assyrian king, speaks of Manasseh as one of the 'servants who belongs to me'. During his reign, religious practices associated with Canaan revived and he is described as killing many innocent people in Jerusalem. The brief reign of Amon (642–640 B.C.) brought no change.

Josiah's reign (640–609 B.C.) inaugurated vigorous moves toward national independence. Assyrian imperial control had been challenged successfully by both Babylon and Egypt. Nabopolassar seized power in Babylon about 627 B.C. Josiah took advantage of this to restore Israel's independence in worship and politics (2 Kings 22–3). The Medes joined Babylon in destroying Nineveh in 612 B.C. (Nahum 1: 12 – 3: 19). They finished the destruction of Assyrian power in 609 B.C.

It was as Pharaoh Necho of Egypt moved to help the beleaguered Assyrian forces that Josiah was killed at Megiddo trying to stop their advance (2 Kings 23: 29). The event brought Judah briefly under Egyptian domination until Babylon defeated Necho at Carchemish in 605 B.C. Judah continued an uneasy existence on the frontier of big-power conflict. Babylon fought an inconclusive battle on Egypt's border in 601 and turned on Jerusalem in 598 B.C. The city's surrender let the king and high officials, along with much treasure, be taken prisoner to Babylon. Continued agitation over the next ten years brought the armies back to destroy the city completely in 587 B.C.

Judah was taken into exile, leaving only a few people living in the ruins of Jerusalem and her villages. The prophets Jeremiah and Ezekiel interpreted the event to Israel as the LORD's judgement on her sin and rebellion. Israel's historians used the story of these rebellions to write a history of the nation. They interpreted the events according to the covenant book of Deuteronomy (that is, that when Israel was faithful to God he would bless her, but when she was unfaithful, he would punish her). Their history recounted Israel's acts of disobedience from the time of her wandering to the periods of the judges and the kings. This history comprises the books of Joshua to 2 Kings.

THE FIFTH CENTURY IN JUDAH

The Persian conquest of Babylon opened the door to Judah's return in 538 B.C. The powerful preaching of the Babylonian Isaiah (Isa. 40–55), Haggai and Zechariah prepared the way for restoration. The temple was finally standing again in the ruins of Jerusalem in 515 B.C.

But the following decades were difficult. Information on the period is sparse. The only direct reference is found in Ezra 4. The report reflects opposition towards Jerusalem from neighbouring district governors including growing tension with those in Samaria. Conflicting interests could be felt in Jerusalem as well.

Persia ruled its empire with power and dispatch. It tolerated no hint of rebellion. Palestine witnessed the repeated march of its armies trying to keep Egypt in its dominion. This century brought increasing struggles with Greek city-states for the control of Asia Minor, the Aegean Islands, and even for Greece itself.

Persian power was often concealed in the velvet glove of political conciliation and skilled administration. She showed real understanding for the religious preferences of subject peoples, including Israel.

With the temple complete, Jewish unity had a symbol. The scattered communities of Jews throughout the ancient world looked again to 'their homeland', 'their city', the city of God: Jerusalem.

The book of Malachi probably reflects conditions of this time. It is less optimistic and idealistic than the sixth-century prophets had been. It complains of lack of faith and of social and political problems. Worship seems to have been at a low ebb. The people were depressed and discouraged.

The dates for Obadiah and Joel will probably fall in this period also. Jonah may belong here or in the latter half of the century.

In 445 B.C. Nehemiah appeared bringing reform and order to Jerusalem. Despite opposition from Sanballat, governor of Samaria, Nehemiah with the blessing of the emperor rebuilt the city walls, reformed the city administration and laid the foundation for a united and functioning Judaism. There were growing communities of Jews in many parts of the world. They were essentially different in form and purpose. Some, like those in Elephantine (Egypt) whose existence archaeology has brought to light, sought to maintain relations with Samaria or Bethel after they were snubbed by Jerusalem. But with Nehemiah, the foundation of Jerusalem's integrity and influence was firmly laid.

More of the history of this period can be found in the companion volume of this series, *Understanding the Old Testament*.

✠ ✠ ✠ ✠ ✠ ✠ ✠ ✠ ✠ ✠ ✠ ✠ ✠

JOEL

✶ ✶ ✶ ✶ ✶ ✶ ✶ ✶ ✶ ✶ ✶ ✶ ✶

POSITION IN THE CANON

Joel stands second in the Twelve Prophets between Hosea and Amos. Because these prophets lived in the eighth century B.C. many readers assume that Joel also belonged to that period. The lack of a date in the title must have been a problem for the editors of the Twelve Prophets.

Joel was probably placed here because he echoes phrases from other prophets, particularly Amos. Compare 3 : 16a with Amos 1 : 2a and 3 : 18a with Amos 9 : 13b. Joel's announcements of judgement on Tyre, Philistia, and Edom parallel those of Amos in 1 : 8–12.

A LITURGY AND A BOOK

Some interpreters have found Joel to be 'literary prophecy', that is, prophecy composed to be read. Others have understood it as a 'liturgy', a prophecy intended for use in public worship.

The book owes its outline and its passion to the dramatic movement of ritual. Its phrases, forms, pictures, and meaning derive from liturgical formulations. It is possible that these were simply borrowed from temple liturgy or that they imitated liturgical forms. But it is much more plausible and helpful to think of the book's first form as one intended to be spoken on the occasion of a great festival.

The work proved much too important to be limited to that one occasion. It was preserved and edited to be read. It proved its genuine prophetic inspiration to its readers, so that it earned its place in the canon of the prophetic books of the Bible.

PLACE IN ISRAEL'S WORSHIP

Joel is clearly a public prophecy, not a private oracle. Its place in developing Israelite worship is therefore of importance.

Joel's work fits a time in which worship associated with the covenant between God and Israel is vital and vigorous. The use of words and phrases related to worship testify to this. The struggle against an unworthy or false worship in the book appears to be aimed at the mixture of heathen practices which had survived the reform efforts of Hezekiah (about 700 B.C.), Josiah (about 625 B.C.) and others, before finally being eliminated by the rigorous reforms of Ezra (between 445 and 400 B.C.).

The clearest association with worship is the repeated reference to 'the day of the LORD'. The high day of the autumn festival was the occasion for much of prophecy's best work from the time of Amos on. Joel relates his message to it. In so doing he provides one of the most important interpretations of it in the Bible.

The celebration of 'the day' in Israel's worship apparently disappeared when Ezra eliminated all worship forms not required by pentateuchal law.

THE DATE OF JOEL

Though precise dating for the book is impossible, the most appropriate time for it is the first half of the fifth century B.C. Some interpreters have placed it earlier and some later. But in this period it joins Obadiah, the last chapters of Isaiah, Zech. 9–14, and Malachi as great expressions of liturgical prophecy. It is the period of the second temple between the revival of Haggai and Zechariah and the reforms of Ezra.

JOEL'S PREDECESSORS

Joel's use and application of classical prophecy makes his work completely at home in the prophetic canon. He has affinities with Amos, Isaiah, Zephaniah, Jeremiah, and Ezekiel. He learned from them and effectively used the same themes and doctrines. He shared the same urgent sense of God's dynamic action in history, of God's zeal for his covenant people, and of God's demand for unmixed allegiance from them.

But the form which Joel's prophecy takes is closer to the liturgical prophecies of Malachi, Zech. 9–14, and Pss. 79 and 120. He seems to belong to the same liturgical traditions that they do, although he may precede them in time. He announces God's direct intervention in a specific situation with an assurance like that of Haggai and Zechariah.

✻   ✻   ✻   ✻   ✻   ✻   ✻   ✻   ✻   ✻   ✻   ✻   ✻

THE TITLE

1 The word of the LORD which came to Joel son of Pethuel.

✻ *The word of the LORD:* the most distinctive description possible for the content of prophecy heads the book. It claims that God is the source of the message and that the prophet has received the divine word. *came* describes how the word was inspired. It may be translated more dynamically as 'happened to'.

Joel son of Pethuel: the form of the title is common to several other books, but identifying the prophet simply by his father's name is found only here and in Jonah. The lack of historical identification with date and place fits the nature of the book. It does not need that to be understood and applied. The book forms a liturgy which could be repeated and re-applied. This makes the listing of places and dates not only unnecessary but even a hindrance to its purpose. The name *Joel* means 'Yahweh is God'. It is a confession of faith made either by a prophet when he chose the name or by his father who named him. He is one of the line of prophets who were faithful to the LORD, exclusive worshippers of the God of Moses and Sinai who had revealed himself as 'Yahweh'. Since reverence for the name of God led to its being un-pronounced, the divine name is known only by its consonants: YHWH. A probable pronunciation is indicated by the spelling Yahweh. Jewish tradition required the substituting of a title, commonly 'LORD', so printed in the N.E.B. to indicate that it represents the divine name. ✶

The day of the LORD

✶ After its brief title the first part of the book (1: 2 – 2: 17) announces a remarkable event (1: 2–4), calls for lamentation from all groups in the house of the LORD (1: 5–14) and leads them in themes of lamentation (1: 15–20). The section moves beyond lament to announce the significance of these events. They are a sign that 'the day of the LORD has come' (2: 1–11). All the people are called to repent (2: 12–17). ✶

THE LOCUSTS

Listen, you elders;   2
hear me, all you who live in the land:
has the like of this happened in all your days
    or in your fathers' days?
Tell it to your sons and they may tell theirs;   3
    let them pass it on from generation to generation.
What the locust has left the swarm eats,   4
    what the swarm has left the hopper eats,
    and what the hopper has left the grub eats.

✻ 2. *elders* are the village or town leaders. In early Hebrew history elders were the heads of clans within the tribes. During the monarchy they were responsible for local government. They had a prominent place in the restored community after the exile. The verse appeals to their age and length of experience: *in all your days*. The event to which the prophecy refers is so extraordinary that they are challenged to remember anything like it. The prophet is sure that they will not be able to recall anything from their own experience or from what has been told them by their parents.

3. This is noteworthy enough to be passed on to children and grandchildren as the most amazing and devastating experience of a lifetime. This second appeal is to all the inhabitants of the country, for the crisis affects everyone.

4. The facts of the matter appear at last. A plague of locusts has devoured the plants, the foliage, and everything green. Four names for *locust* are used which apparently describe stages in its life-cycle: each more destructive than the one before. *locust* is the most common term, referring to the mature insect. Three earlier stages are the *grub*, for the larva stage; the *hopper*, for the devouring or nymphal stage; and the *swarm*, for the final or winged stage. The entire process of development may take as much as three years.

The locust plagues which hit Palestine usually come from Sudan. The eggs are deposited in moist soil. When conditions are right, millions of them are laid. The hatched grubs, driven by hunger, move across the land in hordes, eating and evolving as they travel. In the winged stage they fly as much as 1000 miles in search of food.

The prophet is apparently describing an actual event. His picture is vivid enough to be from an eye-witness. He assumes that the people know exactly what he is talking about because they, too, have experienced the disaster. He will interpret the plagues as one aspect of 'the day of the LORD'. But before doing that, he calls on various groups to respond to the disaster. ✻

LAMENT

Wake up, you drunkards, and lament your fate;   5
mourn for the fresh wine, all you wine-drinkers,
    because it is lost to you.
For a horde has overrun my land,   6
    mighty and past counting;
    their teeth are a lion's teeth;
    they have the fangs of a lioness.
They have ruined my vines   7
and left my fig-trees broken and leafless,
they have plucked them bare
and stripped them of their bark;
    they have left the branches white.

✻ 5–6. The effects of the locust plague are shown in its results. The message is being spoken in autumn, at or near the usual time for the harvest of grapes, olives, and figs. This means that the locusts did their work shortly before the pilgrim festival of Ingathering (Exod. 23: 16) which was celebrated in the autumn. Being a harvest festival, there was usually drinking of the new wine in celebration. But the people would go thirsty this year. *horde* is literally 'a nation'. It is applied to ants and rock-badgers in Prov. 30:25–7. Joel uses the word to compare the locusts to an invading army, *mighty and past counting*. The metaphor of invasion is continued in 2: 2–11.

The second half of verse 6 is a good example of the Hebrew poetic form known as parallelism. Two lines say the same thing in slightly different ways: *lion's teeth* and *fangs of a lioness*.

7. The locusts not only strip away leaves and fruit from trees and vines. They *stripped them of their bark* and undoubtedly killed many plants in the process. ✻

CALL TO MOURNING

8   Wail like a virgin wife in sackcloth,
      wailing over the bridegroom of her youth:
9   the drink-offering and grain-offering are lost
      to the house of the LORD.
   Mourn, you priests, ministers of the LORD,
10   the fields are ruined, the parched earth mourns;
   for the corn is ruined, the new wine is desperate,
      the oil has failed.
11   Despair, you husbandmen; you vinedressers, lament,
      because the wheat and the barley,
      the harvest of the field, is lost.
12   The vintage is desperate, and the fig-tree has failed;
      pomegranate, palm, and apple,
      all the trees of the country-side are parched,
      and none make merry over harvest.

13   Priests, put on sackcloth and beat your breasts;
      lament, you ministers of the altar;
   come, lie in sackcloth all night long, you ministers of
      my God;
      for grain-offering and drink-offering
   are withheld from the house of your God.
14   Proclaim a solemn fast, appoint a day of abstinence.
      You elders, summon all that live in the land
      to come together in the house of your God,
      and cry to the LORD.
15   Alas! the day is near,
   the day of the LORD: it comes,
   a mighty destruction from the Almighty.
16   Look! it stares us in the face;

the house of our God has lost its food,
>lost all its joy and gladness.
>The soil is parched,   17
>the dykes are dry,
>the granaries are deserted,
>the barns ruinous;
>for the rains have failed.
>The cattle are exhausted,   18
>the herds of oxen distressed
because they have no pasture;
the flocks of sheep waste away.
To thee I cry, O LORD;   19
>for fire has devoured the open pastures
and the flames have burnt up all the trees of the
>country-side.
The very cattle in the field look up to thee;   20
>for the water-channels are dried up,
>and fire has devoured the open pastures.

✻ 8. The prophecy appeals for mourning. Israel, having lost her harvest, is compared to a child-bride, so frequent in the East, who is widowed before she can even be a wife. She is called to mourn accordingly.

9*a*. Food is scarce enough for daily offerings in the temple to be suspended. These offerings included a lamb sacrificed each morning and evening in addition to grain-offerings, olive oil and wine. But now there is no grain-offering because all vegetation had been destroyed. Such offerings were symbols of Israel's vital communion with God. To stop them introduced a spiritual crisis.

9*b*–10. So the *priests* who usually offered the sacrifices are called to join the *fields* that are *ruined* and the *parched earth* in their mourning. When locusts strip plants and trees, they die.

The ground no longer has their roots to hold moisture and it dries up into dust. It would take years of patient work to repair the damage. The results are succinctly summarized in terms of the harvest's usual products: *corn – ruined*; *new wine – desperate*; *oil* from olives *– failed*.

11. Workers in the fields are called to join the mourning. Unemployment adds to the problems of hunger, thirst, and discontinued religious services. *wheat* and *barley* are not harvested at that time. They would normally be planted at the first rains of autumn. But the situation appears desperate for them as well, for a drought complicates problems caused by the locusts (cp. 1: 17–20; 2: 3). Locusts flourish during dry periods. Drought and locusts combine to be as complete a catastrophe for the agricultural community as one can imagine.

12. *harvest* was normally a happy time of rejoicing and thanksgiving. But the ruin of tree culture, including *pomegranate*, *palm* and *apple*, had robbed them of any reason for merriment (cp. comments on Hab. 3: 17).

13. A new section begins and the call to mourning takes on a more formal character. What the fields do, the workers reflect, and the consumers decry, must be represented in formal religious rites in *the house of your God*. Mourning rites called for priests to replace their splendid ceremonial robes with rough sackcloth, their grand rites of sacrifice, praise, and thanksgiving with elemental forms of penance and mourning: hence *beat your breasts…lie in sackcloth all night long*. The services of the temple are sensitive to the conditions of life among the people. They are dependent for gifts and offerings on the well-being of the people. They are also intended to represent the needs of the people in prayers to God.

ministers refers to the priests as persons of high appointed position. These high officials are called to humble themselves in mourning. A progression is evident in the relation to God of the groups addressed. The prophet summons the priests to action as *ministers of my God* with the reminder that the drought affects the offerings at *the house of your God*.

14. The call to the *elders* to extend the mourning to all the people is connected to *the house of your God*, that is, the God of the elders and the people. The progression is clearer still in Hebrew which reads 'the house of the LORD your God'. The relation to God of the prophet, the priests, the elders, and the people is brought to a climax by the name of God, Yahweh, particularly associated with the covenant which binds them all. *a solemn fast* is appropriate both because it so directly reflects the problems of hunger and because it is considered a correct way to approach God in a time of judgement (cp. Jonah 3: 7–9).

This and the following part of the prophecy are structured like the 'communal lament' found in many Psalms (e.g. Ps. 60). It has a call to assemble (1: 13–14), lamentations (1: 15–18), and supplications (1: 19–20).

15. In this verse Joel's distinctive message is spoken: the locusts and drought are signs that *the day of the LORD* is near. *the day* is understood to be one of destruction and judgement. Amos referred to 'the day' as one familiar to the people of his time. On that day the LORD approached his people bringing light and the promise of blessing. As such 'the day' had a fixed place in Israel's religious calendar. Amos reminded the people that the LORD's near presence could have fearful consequences instead of the blessings they had come to expect. He preached that Israel's sin and indifference would in fact make the LORD's visitation one of judgement rather than approval (Amos 5: 18–20). Joel's preaching follows the same line as that of Amos and the similar tone of Zephaniah (1: 7, 14–16), though at a much later time. It may be that one of the festival days was still celebrated as the day of the LORD's coming. The people could hope that the day would bring blessing fulfilling his promises for his people and his land. Joel seizes upon the locust plague to preach that the LORD's coming at this time will be *a mighty destruction from the Almighty*.

Joel's announcement, *the day of the LORD...is near*, is like that of John the Baptist and of Jesus, 'the kingdom of God is upon you' (Mark 1: 15; cp. Matt. 3: 2). In both, the time of the coming is a problem for the translators. The Hebrew language, and perhaps the people too, were not very time-conscious. The tenses in English are clearly past, present, or future. But those in Hebrew represent completed or incompleted acts, each of which may be thought of in past, present, or future contexts without changing the form of the verb. This forces the translator to decide in each case from the context whether a particular Hebrew verb should be put into an English past, present, or future tense though the Hebrew could possibly be any or all of these.

The theme for Joel is that this terrible day *is near*, has been decided upon, is even at that moment breaking upon the people. The message is typically prophetic, in the proper sense, for it speaks of what is present or in the immediate future, which demands a decision from the people now.

16–18. The disastrous situation which *stares* them *in the face* is depicted again. The temple has no offerings and lacks *joy and gladness*, those qualities of which the Psalms sing so often. The devastation of the *soil* follows the failure of *the rains*. The empty reservoirs make *dry...dykes*. With nothing to store, *granaries* and *barns* go to ruin. Palestine has a climate clearly divided into dry and rainy seasons. It expects no rain from April to September. So it must get enough moisture during the other half-year to survive. If a drought deprives it of rain in the normally 'rainy season', the prospect is bleak indeed. This is the picture Joel gives, *for the rains have failed*. Domestic animals join in the suffering of the soil caught in the grip of drought. They have neither water to drink nor *pasture* to feed on.

19. The prophet pleads with the LORD for the parched land. *fire* has added its destruction at the very time when everything is already so dry that it burns easily.

20. The *cattle* join the prophet's appeal for relief from the drought. ✳

ALARM

Blow the trumpet in Zion,   **2**
sound the alarm upon my holy hill;
let all that live in the land tremble,
   for the day of the LORD has come,
surely a day of darkness and gloom is upon us,   2
   a day of cloud and dense fog;
like a blackness spread over the mountains
a mighty, countless host appears;
their like has never been known,
nor ever shall be in ages to come;
their vanguard a devouring fire,   3
their rearguard leaping flame;
before them the land is a garden of Eden,
behind them a wasted wilderness;
nothing survives their march.
On they come, like squadrons of horse,   4
like war-horses they charge;
bounding over the peaks they advance with the rattle 5
   of chariots,
like flames of fire burning up the stubble,
like a countless host in battle array.
Before them nations tremble,   6
every face turns pale.
  Like warriors they charge,   7
  they mount the walls like men at arms,
each marching in line,
  no confusion in the ranks,
none jostling his neighbour,   8
none breaking line.

They plunge through streams without halting their
advance;
9 they burst into the city, leap on to the wall,
climb into the houses,
entering like thieves through the windows.
10 Before them the earth shakes,
the heavens shudder,
sun and moon are darkened,
and the stars forbear to shine.
11 The LORD thunders before his host;
his is a mighty army,
countless are those who do his bidding.
Great is the day of the LORD and terrible,
who can endure it?

✡ This section describes the locusts themselves rather than the destruction they have caused. The harm to fields and pastures was pictured in the first chapter. Now the city is attacked.

1. *the trumpet* is the Hebrew *shōphār* or ram's horn. It was used as a signal for battle, for movement of a large number of people, and for alarm. In worship it signalled the coming of the LORD. Joel combines its use as a warning with the signal of the LORD's coming. *my holy hill* is Zion, the place of the temple in Jerusalem. To *tremble* is understood to show the 'fear of the LORD', a basic response to his presence and his holiness. *for:* the reason for alarm and for awe goes beyond the calamity at hand to its ultimate cause. *the day of the LORD* continues to be the theme, picking up the thread of thought from 1: 15 and following it in 2: 10–11. *has come* translates a verb which may also mean 'is coming'. The Hebrew text adds the phrase 'for it is near' which is correctly judged by the N.E.B. to be a redundant addition. It is apparently a

copyist's note to ensure a rendering in present time (cp. the comment on 1: 15).

2. *darkness and gloom* are fitting figures for the judgement of that great day. Amos had warned that there would be darkness rather than light (Amos 5: 18). Joel skilfully blends the imagery of prophecy with the realistic experience of the locust plague. Travellers who have seen such confirm the accuracy of the account. Locust swarms darken the sky like an eclipse of the sun; at dusk the low rays of the sun catch their wings, reflecting an eerie light. *host* is a military term. The locusts are like an invading army. *fire* is an apt metaphor for the locusts' destructive power. It was used in 1: 19, either literally or figuratively, in relation to the drought. It is fitting in both places. *nothing survives their march* is literally true of all green things in the path of locusts.

4. *war-horses:* older commentaries have understood this comparison to horses to refer to the speed of movement and the formation of the ranks of locusts. An old Arab proverb says: 'In the locust is the face of a horse, the eyes of an elephant, the neck of a bull, the horns of a deer, the chest of a lion, the belly of a scorpion, the wings of an eagle, the thighs of a camel, the feet of an ostrich, and the tail of a serpent.'

5. The sounds of locusts are *the rattle of chariots*...*the burning* of *stubble*. Modern descriptions compare them to the sound of heavy rain in a forest, the distant rumble of waves, the rattle of hail or the crackling of a bush on fire.

6. Modern pest controls are hardly adequate to deal with such a plague. Ancient peoples were helpless before it.

7–9. With something almost like admiration Joel recounts the disciplined and determined march of the locusts. Even *streams* are no barriers to their advance. An eye-witness reported a plague in Lebanon in 1845: 'We dug trenches and kindled fires, and beat and burned to death heaps upon heaps, but the effort was utterly useless. Wave after wave rolled up the mountains, and poured down upon us, over rocks, walls, ditches and hedges, those behind covering up and bridging over the masses already killed.'

10. *the earth shakes, the heavens shudder:* figures which had traditionally been thought part of 'the day of the LORD' are seen to be literally fulfilled in the plague. It is understood to be an act of God and a beginning of the great judgement.

11. Some of the oldest passages in the Old Testament (cp. Num. 10: 35) portray God leading his people out to battle, going before them, even fighting in their stead. Joel sees the locusts as God's destructive army. Their discipline and determined advance is due to God's personal leadership. But the description leaves the impression also that the locusts are only a symbol of the true *mighty army* which the LORD commands. *the day of the LORD* has a sinister meaning for the prophet. Its darkness and calamities are anticipated by the ravaging locusts. He cries out that it is *Great* and *terrible* and asks, *who can endure it?*, because of the recent impression made by the locust plague. ✻

INVITATION TO REPENT

12   And yet, the LORD says, even now
　　　turn back to me with your whole heart,
　　　fast, and weep, and beat your breasts.

13   Rend your hearts and not your garments;
　　　turn back to the LORD your God;
　　　for he is gracious and compassionate,
　　　　　long-suffering and ever constant,
　　　always ready to repent of the threatened evil.

14   It may be he will turn back and repent
　　　and leave a blessing behind him,
　　　　　blessing enough for grain-offering and drink-
　　　　　　offering
　　　　　for the LORD your God.

26

Blow the trumpet in Zion,   15
proclaim a solemn fast, appoint a day of abstinence;
gather the people together, proclaim a solemn assembly;   16
  summon the elders,
gather the children, yes, babes at the breast;
  bid the bridegroom leave his chamber
    and the bride her bower.
  Let the priests, the ministers of the LORD,   17
  stand weeping between the porch and the altar
and say, 'Spare thy people, O LORD, thy own people,
  expose them not to reproach,
  lest other nations make them a byword
  and everywhere men ask,
    "Where is their God?"'

✻ 12. *And yet* marks the turning point in the prophet's
message. It is typical of the offer of grace and forgiveness
which is the good news of the Bible. *the LORD says:* the offer
of pardon and a reversal of events is made by God himself.
He alone has the authority to offer it. *even now:* although the
locusts have already wrought havoc and 'the day of the
LORD' is at hand, it is not too late for total disaster to be
averted. *turn:* the literal meaning of repentance is a change of
direction. The implication is that Israel has had its back to
God and was moving away from him and his way of life.
He invites them to *turn back* to him. *heart* in the Old Testament
is understood to be the seat of the will and the intellect, rather
than the modern idea connecting it with the emotions. God
calls for repentance which is a complete decision accompanied
by signs of penance: *fast…weep, and beat your breasts.*

13. God calls for more than outward expressions of repentance. Tearing *garments* was a common form of mourning.
Rend your hearts demands breaking up patterns of decision and

conduct, a change in the way you think about things and decide matters. To *turn back to the LORD* as *your God* means to shape your life style in such a way as to show who your God is, to choose between alternate possibilities according to his will.

for begins the explanation of the reason why the prophet can confidently proclaim this contrasting possibility of mercy if the people repent. What follows is a short statement of faith which is also found in Jonah 4: 2. Both are drawn from God's revelation of himself to Moses on Sinai (Exod. 34: 6). *gracious and compassionate* are warm terms of tender feeling like those of a mother for her child. *long-suffering* is literally 'long of nostrils' meaning that one is slow-breathing and hence slow to anger. *ever constant* translates words which show great loyalty and devotion to those who are related to one as Israel is related to the LORD in covenant. *repent* when used of God does not imply sorrow for having done wrong. He will change his mind or intention. He turns around. Even with this clear, it is a shocking statement: *always ready to repent of the threatened evil*. Jonah rebelled against this basic tenet of Israel's faith (cp. Jonah 4: 2). But this is the essence of good news from God for any generation. It explains the 'And yet' of verse 12.

14. Since God is 'always ready to repent of the threatened evil', *It may be* that he will do so again. For the LORD to *turn back* will change the curse of judgement into *blessing*. It will make his day 'light' instead of darkness. Rain will avert the drought and he will turn back the locusts, healing the wounds they have inflicted on the land. The LORD's presence on that day would be welcome and beneficial, rather than dreadful and destructive. But this good possibility depends on having the people turn back to God. *blessing enough:* offerings to God depend upon having more food than is required for the elemental needs of the people. Worship and offering are possible for men because God has already blessed. The prophet implies that repentance now will make thankful and joyous

worship possible in the future. *the LORD your God* implies a healthy relation between God and his people which comes when they have turned back to recognize him as their God. This was the goal of the Sinai covenant. God said then that Israel would be his people and he would be their God when they kept his covenant.

15. *Blow the trumpet in Zion* repeats the command of 2: 1. But the purpose is no longer to sound an alarm but to call the people to *a solemn fast* which the prophet had ordered the priests to proclaim in 1: 14. The wording here is identical. A *fast* and *abstinence* from food were appropriate signs for penance and for mourning.

16. *solemn assembly* is a special meeting of the people such as here for a public fast. They must prepare for it with ritual purification.

17. *the priests* are addressed by the high title of *the ministers of the LORD*. They are the appointed functionaries of God's court. The prophet calls on them to stand at a distance from the altar in recognition of the breach in relations to God and to weep publicly as they plead for God's mercy. They are to appeal on the grounds of God's special relation to Israel. *thy own people* refers to Israel's understanding of herself as a chosen people. God had chosen Abraham and the generations after him to be a special people for himself (Gen. 15). In order to fulfil this he had rescued Israel from Egypt and made a covenant with her at Sinai. All of this provides the overtones for *thy people* and the particular appeal to God. The Hebrew has different words here. The first 'people' carries all the meaning of the covenant. The second is literally 'thy possession' or 'inheritance' and heightens the meaning even more. Yet all the teaching of being the chosen people did not take the place of faithful obedience to the covenant on the part of the people. Because they had forgotten this the crisis had arisen. Only repentance and return can set things right again.

lest other nations: Israel's recognition that the LORD who had chosen her was also the God of all the world made her see her position in another light. It was not only grace and compassion that motivated his relation to her. He intended that Israel's existence should be a witness to himself before the peoples and nations. Moses appealed for God's patience with his people on this basis (Exod. 32: 12; Num. 14: 13–16). Ezekiel used it for a sermon (Ezek. 20). And it occurs in prayers of the community after the exile (Pss. 42: 4; 79: 10; 115: 2). If Israel were destroyed in the judgement, the peoples would conclude that God does not exist or is not strong enough to protect his own. But the very fact that Israel through repentance recognizes that she is God's people and, as such, has a place in his relation to the world is a reason for mercy and a new beginning on God's part.

These words are spoken to the Jerusalem congregation. To them Joel cries: 'Who can endure the day of the LORD?' Amos (5: 18–20) and Isaiah (2: 9–22) had preached that it was impossible to flee from the LORD's anger. So Joel calls the people to 'turn back to' him instead of fleeing from him. No specific sins or failures, whether social, political, or religious, are mentioned in this chapter. Repentance is not so much a turning from sin as a turning to God. It means that people should come to count seriously on the God of the preached word as the one who will come. It means that people should not be content with simply seeing to it that worship services continued to function, but that under the preaching of the prophetic word they would wait for God's coming which will prove beyond doubt his rule over the world. Jerusalem's situation in Joel's time was such that its continued existence depended upon a new sign of his mercy.

Centuries later Jerusalem met Jesus Christ with this call of Joel in her ears. His coming brought a division in her people. Some were content to continue in their religious practices, primarily obedience to the law of Moses. Some heeded the call of Joel and others like him who looked expectantly for the new act of God's mercy. The first group fell under the power of heathen nations and down the centuries some con-

tinued faithful in adherence to the Law. The second found in
Christ a rich heritage of blessing in which they saw a fulfilment
of ancient promise. The message of Joel continues to be
relevant. Many people still think of the maintenance of
worship as the goal of faith. But the LORD's message is about
the emancipation of all men. He is yet to come to complete
that work. Faith and repentance mean to count on his coming
and to turn one's hope towards the coming LORD. In this the
message of Joel has lost nothing of its pertinence and power. ✶

Israel forgiven and restored

✶ This is the turning point in the book of Joel. The first part
was a call to prayer for God's mercy and help in a time of
distress because 'the day of the LORD' was near. The part that
follows documents God's response to that prayer. It assures
new life for all who call upon the LORD.

It begins with narrative (2: 18–19*a*) which is parallel to
the description of the locust plague in 1: 6–7. The return of
rain and of material blessings is assured in a series of messages
(2: 19–20, 21–4, 25–7). A second series of three promises
spiritual blessing and salvation for all the faithful (2: 28–9,
30–1, 32). This announcement of salvation returns to the
theme of 'the day'. With this, the issue of Judah's and Israel's
security among the nations is raised. God assures them that
he will go on living in Zion and that those who call on him
and are called by him will be secure there. Ch. 3 gives a
description of 'the day of the LORD' in terms of judgement
over the nations, a judgement which will ensure Jerusalem's
and Judah's survival. ✶

GOD'S ANSWER

18   Then the LORD's love burned with zeal for his land,
         and he was moved with compassion for his people.
19   He answered their appeal and said,
     I will send you corn, and new wine, and oil,
         and you shall have your fill;
     I will expose you no longer
         to the reproach of other nations.
20   I will remove the northern peril far away from you
     and banish them into a land parched and waste,
         their vanguard into the eastern sea
           and their rear into the western,
     and the stench shall rise from their rotting corpses
         because of their proud deeds!

✳ 18. The shift to narrative is marked and clear. The prophet is no more than a messenger from the LORD. A change in the prophet's message depends on a prior change in the LORD's decision. This change, which was thought a bare possibility in verse 14, has in fact taken place. *the LORD's love burned with zeal* is a paraphrase; more literally the words mean 'become jealous'. The reference is to that special and exclusive claim which God makes on his people. Because of his great love, he is fired with jealous anger. The word is a strong one expressing the intensity of God's concern.

God's *land* and his *people* are the objects of his *zeal* and *compassion*. The way that the land and the people are related may be traced back to the promises to Abraham in Gen. 13:14–18; 17: 6–8 and to the book of Joshua.

19. *answered* is the key to the nature of the second half of the book. The first part presented the need and the *appeal* to God. The second is God's answer to that plea. The Hebrew is in fact repetitive here, literally: 'so the LORD answered and

said to his people'. The sentences stress God's response to his people's repentance and prayers. They also emphasize the essentials of the covenant relation: the LORD in dialogue with his people through their worship. *I will send:* the Hebrew uses a vivid idiom, very common in prophetic speech and expressing what will happen in the immediate future: 'behold me sending to you'. God's answer is given in deeds which will relieve their distress and restore the bounty of their harvests. At the same time what he does will take away *the reproach of other nations* who, quite properly, gave Israel's distress a religious interpretation. Now the change in their condition will disprove the contention that Israel's God was powerless or that he had abandoned them completely.

20. *the northern peril:* some interpreters have seen in this a reference to an invader. But the rest of the verse fits the locust plague. Locusts usually come from the south or east to Palestine, so it is unlikely to be a literal reference to their origin. The 'north' is sometimes used to refer to the secret dwelling-place of God, and hence when it is used in reference to judgement, it may carry both the sense of invaders from the north – from Assyria or Babylon – and of supernatural action. The use of the term for the locust invasion reflects the way Joel had already interpreted the plague as a sign that 'the day of the LORD' was near. *eastern sea* must refer to the Persian Gulf while the *western* would be the Mediterranean Sea. The scene is very broad. It fits the great drama of 'the day' better than the specific problems of the locusts.

This first answer had been spoken by the LORD himself, promising his intervention to restore their food-supply and eliminate the twin problems of drought and locusts. ✳

A CALL TO RESPOND

Earth, be not afraid, rejoice and be glad;   21
    for the LORD himself has done a proud deed.
    Be not afraid, you cattle in the field;   22

for the pastures shall be green,
the trees shall bear fruit,
the fig and the vine yield their harvest.

23   O people of Zion,
rejoice and be glad in the LORD your God,
who gives you good food in due measure[a]
and sends down rain[b] as of old.[c]

24   The threshing-floors shall be heaped with grain,
the vats shall overflow with new wine and oil.

✷ The prophet calls for a response from those who benefit from God's goodness: the earth, the cattle, and the people of Zion. The LORD has done a 'proud' or heroic 'deed' which the prophet has ironically put opposite the 'proud deeds' which led to the locusts' destruction.

21. *rejoice and be glad* are words particularly related to harvest. These verses speak of reversing the conditions described in 1: 6–7, 10–12, and 19–20.

23. The *people of Zion* is the worshipping congregation of Israel in Jerusalem. Their rejoicing should be in *the LORD your God* rather than in the blessing itself. This is a warning that is always applicable. It is so much easier to be happy about the gift than to keep one's attention on the giver and the love that motivated the gift.

The rest of the verse is obscure and has given translators much trouble, as the notes in the N.E.B. indicate. But that translation has hidden one clear thing. The second half of the verse tells why the people of Zion should rejoice in the LORD: 'for he has given to you – and has caused rain to descend on you, early and late rains as in the beginning.' The problem is caused by the word which the N.E.B. has changed slightly

[a] *Or* gives you a sign pointing to prosperity.
[b] *Prob. rdg.; Heb. adds* spring rain and autumn rain.
[c] as of old: *so Sept.; Heb.* in the first month.

and translated *good food*. The R.S.V. has 'early rain'. The basic
meaning of the word is 'to throw' or 'sow'. It can have the
meaning of 'archer' or 'teacher'. It is followed by the words
'to righteousness'. Hos. 10: 12 uses these words together
as a figure of teaching being the sowing of truth to bring a
rich harvest. Joel connects the need for a 'teacher for righteousness' with God's providential gifts of rain. The 'teacher of
righteousness' could apply to the prophet himself. God's gift
of a prophet to teach the people their spiritual need and call
them to repentance comes before his gift of rain. The connection of teaching for righteousness and the gift of rain appears
in Hos. 10: 12 and in 1 Kings 8: 36. The Jewish sectarian
writings from Qumran in the first century B.C. speak of a
'Teacher of Righteousness' who was their leader.

as of old (cp. N.E.B. footnote). The difference between
the emended translation and that in the note is a single
letter in Hebrew. 'In the first month' would have been
very meaningful to worshippers in the autumn festival cele-
brating the New Year. They would fear that the drought
and the locusts would continue. Joel appeals to them not
to be afraid, but to have faith that God's word in answer
to their prayers and repentance will be fulfilled. Within
'the first month', the usual time for rains, God will send the
rains again.

24. With the return of rain the promise of full harvests
would be well on the way to being fulfilled. ✶

GOD'S INTERPRETATION

So I will make good the years   25
    that the swarm has eaten,
hopper and grub and locust,
my great army which I sent against you;
    and you shall eat, you shall eat your fill   26
    and praise the name of the LORD your God

who has done wonders for you,[a]
27 and you shall know that I am present in Israel,
that I and no other am the LORD your God;
and my people shall not again be brought to shame.

☆ These verses continue God's statement of his restoration in verses 19–20. God's act for Israel ('I will make good') is followed by three complementary acts by Israel ('you shall eat', 'praise', 'you shall know'). The message closes with the LORD's formal signature and promise.

25. *make good* has the meaning of 'heal' or 'make whole'. *the years:* Joel is sensitive to the total loss from such a period of privation which leaves psychological and physical scars far deeper than the direct effects of famine. God's salvation will be concerned with healing the effects of those lost and 'devoured' years. God recognizes again that the locusts were his own *great army*. He had sent them against his people when they had forgotten him. Now he gladly restores his people since they have turned back to him.

26. This restoration will have three results for God's people. First, it will provide for physical needs: they will *eat* and be satisfied. Second, it will restore genuine worship: they will *praise the name of the LORD* as their own *God* because they will recognize that he *has done wonders* for them. Worship is not simply a means of getting answers to prayers. It is founded in thanksgiving and praise for what God is and has done.

27. The third result will be a new measure of religious consciousness and knowledge. True worship begins with a knowledge of the real presence of God in all of life. To *know* means the perception that comes from experience; this is what Israel gains through the drought and subsequent restoration in response to her faith. *I am present in Israel* is literally 'in the midst of Israel am I'. This literal meaning puts God in the

[*a*] *Prob. rdg.; Heb. adds* and my people shall not again be brought to shame (*cp. verse 27*).

centre of things, whether Israel knew it or not. He made his presence known in the plague. Israel finally recognized him because of the prophet's preaching. Then God revealed his presence by restoring Israel and she was able to respond with praise. This verse effectively answers the taunt of verse 17: 'Where is their God?'

The passage ends with the ceremonial statement in which God introduces himself. *I . . . am the LORD your God* is like the statement which introduces the Ten Commandments (Exod. 20: 2): it is both a comforting assurance and a stern reminder. *and no other:* God does not relinquish his claim to his people to any other god, nor does he allow them to look to any other. This is the other aspect of God's jealousy (cp. note on verse 18); God can have no rival in his people's loyalty.

This entire passage is a message of salvation for the people of God. It closes with the assurance: *my people shall not again be brought to shame. again* is a reference to the destruction of Jerusalem and the exile of its people in 587 B.C. The memory of that dreadful event was very much alive in the minds of the people of Joel's time. God had heard Israel's prayer and turned away the effects of the locust plague and the drought. He will likewise hear their plea to protect them from the threatening 'day of the LORD' and will do so in an equally wonderful way. *

PREPARATION FOR 'THE DAY OF THE LORD'

Thereafter the day shall come 28ᵃ
when I will pour out my spirit on all mankind;
your sons and your daughters shall prophesy,
your old men shall dream dreams
and your young men see visions;
I will pour out my spirit in those days 29
even upon slaves and slave-girls.

[a] *3: 1 in Heb.*

30   I will show portents in the sky and on earth,
          blood and fire and columns of smoke;
31   the sun shall be turned into darkness
              and the moon into blood
      before the great and terrible day of the LORD comes.
32   Then everyone who invokes the LORD by name
              shall be saved:
          for when the LORD gives the word
          there shall yet be survivors on Mount Zion
              and in Jerusalem a remnant[a]
          whom the LORD will call.[b]

✽ God promises that he will make the next period not only as good as the old times (verse 23), but much better.

28. *Thereafter:* this new phase belongs to the future. It presumes that the promises of verses 18–25 have been fulfilled and that Israel does know that the LORD is present in the centre of her life. *the day* is not in the Hebrew. This section does not refer to 'the day of the LORD', but to conditions which precede it. *I will pour out:* the words are those used for pouring water or other liquids. God will let his spirit flow without measure. *spirit* is life-power. It provides the will and the energy for effective action. God controls it and gives it to humans in order for them to live and to make particular acts or skills possible. Without this gift men are unable to do the will of God or to stand up against the powers of evil. When God pours out his spirit *on all mankind* he will be founding a new and powerful form of life. Men who would otherwise be weak and helpless in the coming judgement, will have the moral and physical strength which had until then been only for the gifted few. A hymn from the Qumran community of the first century B.C. illustrates this understanding of the

[a] a remnant: *prob. rdg.; Heb.* among the remnant.
[b] *Or* when the LORD calls.

spirit: 'I thank you, LORD, for you have supported me with your power. You have poured your holy spirit upon me, so that I will not waver. You have strengthened me for the battle with the evil one.'

all mankind will receive the spirit. It is literally 'all flesh'. This does not refer to the nations, but to everyone in Israel without distinction of sex, or age, or social status. This promise fulfils Moses' wish (Num. 11: 29). It envisages a society created by the gift of God's spirit in which the *old* and the *young*, the men and the women, the 'slaves' and the free will share equally in the life-giving and empowering gift of God's spirit.

prophesy...dream...see visions: this is the result of the pouring out of the spirit. But there is no word about the contents, words spoken, or visions seen. The important thing is that they should be prophets, men whose total orientation is toward God and his coming. The gift of the spirit creates a new relation to God which in its immediacy is a witness that God is present (verse 27) and that his day is coming. When Exod. 19: 6f. describes all Israel as priests, it is a parallel picture of this unmediated access to God.

The presence of these spirit-filled prophets leads people to invoke the LORD by name in the day of trouble (verse 32). Joel sees saving faith, not so much in obedience to religious practices and law, as in the prophetic certainty of the coming deeds of God for his people (cp. also Ezek. 39: 29).

30. God will also show *portents* or very extraordinary happenings *in the sky* and *on earth*. These cosmic signs demonstrate the universal significance of 'the day' which includes all creation as well as all history.

31. *sun...into darkness...moon into blood* effectively describes an eclipse. *before* is not simply previous in time, but as facing toward that day. Both the gifts of the spirit and the portents are given in view of the nearness of 'the day' and in preparation for it. That the *day of the LORD* is *great and terrible* was already made clear in verse 11. At that time Israel could

only face it in uncertainty and fear. The locusts and the drought were signs of its destructive force. In contrast these words were intended to bolster a confidence which is founded on the gifts of God's spirit and his portents. It grows out of the experience of answered prayer about the locusts and the assurance that God is 'present in Israel'.

32. No matter how terrible 'the day' may be, *everyone who invokes the LORD by name shall be savied. everyone* for Joel meant all in Israel to whom the holy name had been given. *saved* meant to have safety or escape danger in the crisis which will come upon Jerusalem in that day. *invoke the LORD by name* meant to pray to God using the sacred name that had been revealed to Moses and through him to all Israel. The prophet's preaching and the testimony of spirit-filled people will make this possible.

This verse was taken up in the New Testament church and applied to belief on the name of Jesus Christ (Rom. 10: 13; Acts 2: 21f.). Paul used the verse to show that there was no longer any difference between Jews and Greeks (Rom. 10: 12). He gave a universal meaning to 'everyone'. Peter's sermon at Pentecost (Acts 2: 17–21) used the larger passage (Joel 2: 28–32) to explain the mass conversion and the gift of the spirit on that day. Through Jesus Christ the promises to Israel in Joel are extended to all mankind. The crucifixion and resurrection of Jesus Christ are said to fulfil God's promise of help to Zion to which Joel testifies. To call on the name of Jesus becomes the way to salvation which means peace for the individual, peaceful relationships between the generations, the sexes, social groups, and even the nations. The gift of the Holy Spirit is described as the sign that God is present and active in and for his people.

The translation *for when the LORD gives the word* seems to put the supporting words that follow in future time. But the clause is literally, 'just as the LORD has said'. Joel is quoting earlier prophecies to support his confidence in the security of Israel in Jerusalem. They promise that there will be *survivors* and a *remnant* in *Mount Zion* even after the events of that great and terrible day. *whom the LORD will call:* literally, 'is calling'. The call from God complements, even precedes, the prayers of those seeking salvation. The mutual interaction of 'calling' and 'being called' is pictured throughout the Bible as the mysterious reality of spiritual life. ✶

NATIONS IN THE VALLEY OF THE LORD'S JUDGEMENT

> When that time comes, on that day **3** 1^a
> when I reverse the fortunes of Judah and Jerusalem,
>> I will gather all the nations together 2
>> and lead them down to the Valley of the LORD's
>>> Judgement^b
>> and there bring them to judgement
> on behalf of Israel, my own possession;
>> for they have scattered my people
>> throughout their own countries,
>>> have taken each their portion of my land
>> and shared out my people by lot, 3
>> bartered a boy for a whore,
> and sold a girl for wine and drunk it down.

✶ A more complete support is given here (and in verses 9–17) for the proclamation of salvation in 2: 32.

One feature of 'the day of the LORD' was that he would sit in judgement over the nations around Israel. Usually on this occasion Israel is saved by having God intervene on her behalf. This is the case in Joel. Some descriptions of this judgement called the nations by name and specified their crimes, but others had them appear as a group without names.

[a] *4: 1 in Heb.*
[b] the LORD's Judgement: *Heb.* Jehoshaphat.

This passage (with verses 9–17) belongs to the latter type. Verses 4–8 belong to the former. They seem to have been inserted into the longer account, picking up the idea of 'selling Israelites'. There is no reason why the two forms should not be used together as here.

Descriptions of this kind are regularly introduced with the words 'for behold' (in the Hebrew, but not translated) which alert the hearers or readers to the importance of what follows.

1. *that time:* the Old Testament is not very time-conscious in terms of hours and minutes. But it is sensitive to the importance of special occasions or events in which God is active. This *time* is related to 'the day of the LORD'. *on that day* is literally 'in those days' and refers to events related to 'the day' although not necessarily taking place on 'the day' itself. *reverse the fortunes* reflects the idea that on New Year's day the destiny of the people was determined for the coming season. During the past period Israel has been under judgement. Now the prophet brings the 'good news' that this will be reversed. It will be changed into a period of blessing and security. *Judah and Jerusalem:* earlier parts of the book have spoken of Israel as the people of God, of Zion as the place of worship, and of the hope for survivors in Jerusalem. The emphasis here on Judah and Jerusalem fits the situation after the exile. The other tribes have disappeared from the stage of history. Only Judah remains as heir to the choosing of Israel and her responsibility. Even the destruction and exile of 587 B.C. had been directed only against them. In this verse the reversal of the exile with all its results is announced.

2. *I will gather:* the LORD is in complete control. He summons and decides. *the nations:* whenever Jerusalem's security is mentioned, the fate of the surrounding nations is also a factor. The history of the entire region is of one piece. In judgement on Israel these nations may be summoned against Jerusalem. But here they must stand before the bar of justice on their own account. *the Valley of the LORD's Judgement* (Hebrew 'Jehoshaphat' = Yahweh judges) cannot be located.

Later tradition thought of it as the Kidron Valley near Jerusalem. It serves as a courtroom for the trial of the nations. *bring them to judgement:* the LORD serves as prosecutor *on behalf of Israel* to bring the charges against them. But the LORD is also acting for himself, for Israel is his *own possession.* This means the land as well as the people. Both belong to him. Judah and Jerusalem are a part of this possession and symbolic of the whole of Israel.

Three charges are brought against the nations. First, they had deported many thousands. *scattered* is a word used for ashes. *their own countries:* Assyrian kings carried away Israelite prisoners in 733 and 721 B.C. Nebuchadnezzar, king of Babylon, deported Judaeans in 597 and 587 B.C. All of these, and perhaps other deportations as well, are meant here. Second, they had appropriated to themselves *their portion of my land.* The exile left a land without tenants. Rulers claimed this land for themselves and their people. The LORD considers this a crime against himself, because Israel's land belongs to him. In stealing people and land the nations have transgressed against the LORD himself.

3. Third, they had sold Israelites, God's own *people,* as slaves. *by lot* describes the distribution of prisoners of war by casting lots, or throwing dice. The following two lines show how little worth they attached to their prisoners. These are the charges brought and proved against the nations. Their sentence and punishment is prescribed in verses 9–12. ✳

JUDGEMENT ON TYRE, SIDON AND PHILISTIA

What are you to me, Tyre and Sidon and all the districts of Philistia? Can you pay me back for anything I have done? Is there anything that you can do to me? Swiftly and speedily I will make your deeds recoil upon your own heads; for you have taken my silver and my gold and carried off my costly treasures into your temples;

6 you have sold the people of Judah and Jerusalem to the
   Greeks, and removed them far beyond their own fron-
7 tiers. But I will rouse them to leave the places to which
   you have sold them. I will make your deeds recoil upon
8 your own heads: I will sell your sons and your daughters
   to the people of Judah, and they shall sell them to the
   Sabaeans, a nation far away. The LORD has spoken.

✽ 4. The idea of 'selling' is the occasion for quoting another
prophecy on that theme, now in prose. But this one names
specific city-states rather than 'the nations' in general. *Tyre*
and *Sidon* were important Phoenician cities that flourished
in the fifth and early fourth centuries. Sidon was destroyed by
Artaxerxes III's Persian armies in 343 B.C. Tyre held out
through a long siege before it fell to Alexander the Great, in
332 B.C. Gaza was the main city of the *districts of Philistia*
and it also fell to Alexander in 332. The LORD disdainfully
mocks their weakness before him before announcing judgement in terms of retribution: *I will make your deeds recoil upon
your own heads.*

5. The charge against them is again three-fold. They have
taken God's own *silver* and *gold* as well as *costly treasures*.
Since God views all Israel as his possession, this may refer
to plunder from any part of Israel. It does not necessarily
mean that they come from the temple. *your temples:* the
Hebrew word here may mean any large building, whether
these be temples or palaces. The charge is one of theft, not
desecration.

6. The second charge is that they *sold the people of Judah and
Jerusalem.* This resumes the theme of verse 3. The sale of war-
prisoners as slaves was an issue in the prophecies accusing the
nations beginning in the time of Amos. *to the Greeks:* the
Phoenician cities had a lively trade with Greece in the fifth
century and slaves may well have been a part of that trade.
The dispersion of Jews throughout the eastern Mediterranean

area was due partly to this slave-trade. The crime involved taking them *far beyond their own frontiers*, thus removing them from the cultural and religious influences of Israel.

7. *rouse* means to activate or set in motion. God will start their movement away from *the places to which you have sold them*.

8. God will apply the principle of making their deeds 'recoil on their heads' by having the sons and daughters of the accused sold to Judaeans. *Sabaeans* were an Arabian people with a reputation as slave-traders. The point here is that they came from *far away* in the opposite direction to Greece. The passage closes with the prophetic words, *The LORD has spoken*. ✳

NATIONS IN THE VALLEY OF THE LORD'S JUDGEMENT
(continued)

Proclaim this amongst the nations: 9–12[a]
Declare a holy war, call your troops to arms!
  Beat your mattocks into swords
    and your pruning-hooks into spears.[b]
Rally to each other's help, all you nations round about.
Let the weakling say, 'I am strong',
  and let the coward show himself brave.[c]
  Let all the nations hear the call to arms
    and come to the Valley of the LORD's Judgement;
let all the warriors come and draw near
    and muster there;
    for there I will take my seat
  and judge all the nations round about.
Ply the sickle, for the harvest is ripe;   13
    come, tread the grapes,

[a] *The order of lines in verses 9–12 has been re-arranged in several places.*
[b] Beat...spears: *cp. Isa. 2: 4; Mic. 4: 3.*
[c] and let...brave: *prob. rdg.; Heb. O* LORD *bring down thy warriors.*

for the press is full and the vats overflow;
    great is the wickedness of the nations.
14   The roar of multitudes, multitudes, in the Valley of
        Decision!
    The day of the LORD is at hand
    in the Valley of Decision;
15   sun and moon are darkened
    and the stars forbear to shine.
16   The LORD roars from Zion
    and thunders from Jerusalem;
    heaven and earth shudder,
    but the LORD is a refuge for his people
    and the defence of Israel.

17   Thus you shall know that I am the LORD your God,
    dwelling in Zion my holy mountain;
    Jerusalem shall be holy,
and no one without the right shall pass through her
    again.

✳ The description of nations in the valley of judgement is continued. The accusations made before have been sustained. It is now time to pronounce and implement the judgement. This begins with a call to arms which is at the same time a summons by the divine court.

9–12. *amongst the nations:* Israel is not included. *holy war:* ancient battles were often treated as wars in which God was present with his people in the fight. Israel's conquest of Canaan was thought of in this way. The soldiers prepared for battle by sanctifying and cleansing themselves as they would have done to go to worship. Israel ceased to think of her warfare in these terms after the reign of David. But the prophets revived the symbolism of 'holy war' to describe God's great judgement and this was continued in the Revelation of John (cp. Rev. 19: 14–21) and may be seen also in the Qumran writing 'The War of the Sons of Light and the Sons of Darkness'.

mattocks into swords: this is the opposite of Isa. 2: 4 and Mic. 4: 3. Instead of the great pilgrimage of the nations to Jerusalem in peace that was pictured there, they are summoned to come to war and destruction. They are to come to *the Valley of the LORD's Judgement* (cp. verse 2). Now the LORD serves as judge rather than prosecutor. He takes his seat to *judge all the nations* around Israel.

13. *Ply the sickle:* a decision has been made. The nations are ripe for execution. Figures of harvest are used to picture the carnage, for *great is* their *wickedness*.

14. *the Valley of Decision* is a synonym for 'the Valley of the LORD's Judgement'. God makes the decision. It is not left open to the nations. The scene is parallel to that of devastation by locusts in ch. 1. This is also interpreted as a sign that *The day of the LORD is at hand*. The earliest use of this announcement was probably in the exercise of holy war. If so, Joel's use of the two together is in accordance with very old traditions.

15. Cosmic signs appear like those in 2: 10.

16. Joel takes verses from the beginning of the book of Amos to identify *Zion* and *Jerusalem* as the seat of God's power which makes *heaven and earth shudder*. Affirmations that the LORD is 'present in Israel' (2: 27) and that in all the turmoil of 'the day' *the LORD is a refuge* and *defence* for his people support the proclamation that 'everyone who invokes the LORD by name shall be saved' (2: 32).

17. A word of proof, like that in 2: 27, closes the section. God's judgement passed on the nations will make Israel to *know* the reality of God and that he has committed himself to them. His *dwelling* is *in Zion* among his people. *holy* here means inviolate. God affirms his defence of the city even in the tumultuous events of 'the day of the LORD'. *again:* cp. comment on 2: 27. ✷

47

PROSPERITY FOR JUDAH IN JERUSALEM

18 When that day comes,
  the mountains shall run with fresh wine
  and the hills flow with milk.
 All the streams of Judah shall be full of water,
  and a fountain shall spring from the LORD's house
   and water the gorge of Shittim,
19 but Egypt shall become a desert
  and Edom a deserted waste,
   because of the violence done to Judah
  and the innocent blood shed in her land;
20–21 and I will spill their blood,
   the blood I have not yet spilt.
 Then there shall be people living in Judah for ever,
 in Jerusalem generation after generation;
 and the LORD will dwell in Zion.

✶ This closing passage repeats the basic themes of the book:
nature's bounty restored (verse 18), judgement on the nations
(verses 19–20), and the assurance that Judah and Jerusalem will
continue to be inhabited. Even 'the LORD will dwell in Zion'.
However, the style is different. It is probably an addition to
the book quoting another prophecy on the same themes.

18. *When that day comes* is a phrase frequently used to
introduce a description of 'the day of the LORD'. Two consequences of the previous action are given. The first is the
wonderful undisturbed bounty of nature (cp. Amos 9: 15).
a fountain shall spring from the LORD's house: amid all the
rivers that are full because of abundant rain in that time, a
particular stream will flow because the LORD dwells on Zion.
His presence there will cause the blessings of water to flow
to all (cp. Ezek. 47: 1–12; Ps. 46: 4). *the gorge of Shittim* cannot

be located exactly, but it probably is an extension of the Kidron Valley leading to the Dead Sea.

19. In contrast to Israel's water, *Egypt* and *Edom* become *desert* and *waste*. The second consequence of the LORD's presence on Zion will be that she will gain political freedom. These are traditional enemies and oppressors of Judah. Egypt was so from the beginning of Israel's history and was a continuing threat. Edom was thought of in this way, especially since the fall of Jerusalem in 587 B.C. (cp. the commentary on Obadiah). Both these nations are mentioned frequently in prophecies against the nations. The charge against them is the spilling of *innocent blood. . .in her land*. This probably refers to Edom's actions in 587 (cp. Obad. 9–14) and Egypt's sins may be those recorded in 1 Kings 14: 25 or 2 Kings 23: 29.

20–1. *I will spill their blood:* the purpose of this action is to free *Judah* to be a people living in her own territory undisturbed *for ever. the LORD will dwell in Zion:* this will be true because the LORD, after his battles and judgement, will have taken residence in Jerusalem. *will dwell* is a continuous tense: the LORD 'will go on residing' *in Zion*.

In this chapter Joel's purpose was to make Israel aware of a new act of God which would change the structure of the nations and lead to a renewal of Jerusalem, thus fulfilling earlier prophecy. The New Testament proclaims that the promise of God's coming to dwell in Zion was fulfilled when Jesus came and when the Holy Spirit blessed the preaching of the Christian Gospel. It does this in the very freedom of God which Joel proclaimed in connection with the plague of locusts. Instead of bloody judgement on the nations, God in Jesus Christ took upon himself the guilt of the nations as well as that of Israel. The fulfilment exceeds the prophecy by far!

For the Christian believer the richness and fullness of life for the individual and for society which Joel prophesied has become reality in the new world which Christ founded and which the outpouring of the Holy Spirit brings to life.

The New Testament, like Joel, foresees a future in which 'the sharp sickle' must go through the world (Mark 4: 29; Rev. 14: 14f.; 18: 20; 19: 15). For the people of God who live in a doomed and dying world, it is both a warning and a message of hope. ✻

✻   ✻   ✻   ✻   ✻   ✻   ✻   ✻   ✻   ✻   ✻   ✻   ✻

OBADIAH

✻　✻　✻　✻　✻　✻　✻　✻　✻　✻　✻　✻　✻

This is the shortest book in the Old Testament. It provides no direct information on when it was written. Its contents suggest that it came after the fall of Jerusalem in 587 B.C. but before Edom as a nation disappeared from the stage of history in the first half of the fifth century. A plausible date for the book is the end of the sixth or the beginning of the fifth century B.C.

A LITURGY

The prophecy is probably a part of a much larger ritual for 'the day of the LORD'. It has the form and function of 'foreign prophecy' in that ritual (cp. pp. 5–6). One of the ways in which Jewish worship in Jerusalem celebrated the LORD's universal reign was by depicting his judgement over the nations. These decisions were a way of showing how the LORD ruled Israel and the world.

A part of the book is remarkably like verses in Jeremiah. Compare verses 1–4 with Jer. 49: 14–16 and verses 5 and 6 with Jer. 49: 9, 10. Edom was commonly attacked in prophecies against foreign nations and both passages appear to draw upon this common stock for occasions like this.

God's punishment of Edom was to occur at a time when news was current that a coalition of nations was planning an invasion of Edom. Obadiah declared this to be the LORD's doing. He would guarantee its success in order to punish Edom's perfidious participation in the sack of Jerusalem in 587 B.C.

The judgement would also make possible the return to Palestine of scattered groups of Israelites. Both the punishment and the return were evidences of God's dominion.

✻   ✻   ✻   ✻   ✻   ✻   ✻   ✻   ✻   ✻   ✻   ✻   ✻

Edom's pride and downfall

1[a] The vision of Obadiah: what the Lord GOD has said concerning Edom.

> When a herald was sent out among the nations, crying,
> 'Rouse yourselves;
> let us rouse ourselves to battle against Edom',
> I[b] heard this message from the LORD:

2 Look, I make you the least of all nations,
> an object of contempt.

3 Your proud, insolent heart has led you astray;
> you who haunt the crannies among the rocks,
> making your home on the heights,
> you say to yourself, 'Who can bring me to the ground?'

4 Though you soar as high as a vulture
> and your nest is set among the stars,
> thence I will bring you down.
> This is the very word of the LORD.

✻ 1. The first sentence is the title of the book. *vision* identifies it as a product of prophetic inspiration. *Obadiah* means 'servant or worshipper of the LORD'. It is a common name in the Old

[a] *Verses 1-4: cp. Jer. 49: 14-16.*
[b] *So Sept., cp. Jer. 49: 14; Heb. we.*

Testament, and it is not possible to identify the prophet with any known person of that name. Perhaps it was intended to keep the author anonymous: to identify the work with one of 'the servants of the LORD', i.e. one of the prophets at the temple. The name Malachi, meaning 'my messenger', is similar.

The second part of the sentence identifies the first oracle (verses 1*b*–4) as an authentic word from God. *the Lord GOD:* here the name Yahweh is represented by GOD since it follows a title which has the meaning 'Lord' (cp. note on p. 15).

God's will concerned a specific people, *Edom*, which occupied a country on the south-east border of Judah. Edom was also called Seir, Hor, and Esau. There was no natural boundary between the countries so the line shifted with the relative strength of the two. The highlands of Edom rose south-east of the Dead Sea in three great steps of red sandstone cliffs to more than 5000 feet (1524 metres) above sea-level. It was rugged country and easily fortified. Only in the north and east were there areas for fruitful cultivation. Teman and Bozrah were its cities, or districts. Sela was a fortified mountain retreat.

The Edomites were in full possession of the territory by the time of Israel's exodus from Egypt (Num. 20: 14–21; 21: 4). They were presented as being in some way kin to Israel, or at least, to Judah. A strong tribal organization existed during Jacob's time which probably became a kingdom before this change took place in Israel (Gen. 36: 15–30).

Israel and Edom were friendly neighbours at the beginning, but David's brutal subjection of Edom (2 Sam. 8: 13–14) brought that period to a close. Until that time Edom must have been thought of as Israel's 'elder brother' in being older and stronger. David's action caused the 'elder' to be 'supplanted' by the 'younger' in close historical parallel to the Jacob–Esau story in Genesis (Gen. 25: 22–6).

At the beginning of the sixth century B.C., when Jerusalem was overcome by the Babylonian armies, Edom, Ammon, and Moab were independent states. Writings of the period after the exile bitterly portray the perfidious role Edom played on the occasion. Thus Ps. 137: 7 reads:

> Remember, O LORD, against the people of Edom
>   the day of Jerusalem's fall,
> when they said, 'Down with it, down with it,
>   down to its very foundations!'

(cp. also the note on Joel 3: 19).

Edom disappeared from the stage of history during the first half of the fifth century, but there is no record of how this happened. It is likely that the Edomites were overpowered and plundered by tribes from the Arabian peninsula.

Prophets proclaimed and psalmists sang that Israel's God was the ruler of all nations. They believed that Jerusalem, David's capital city, had been chosen in a special sense as God's dwelling-place where his throne was established. The people knew that he came in spirit, not physically. They worshipped him as the one who spiritually lived in the temple. But they also believed that he expressed his will and acted through the descendant of David on the throne and through his chosen people in Jerusalem, his city.

Prophecies about other nations were made from this point of view. They often included one against their near neighbour, sometime kinsfolk, and frequent enemy, Edom. Thus religious convictions expressed in the temple during worship had their parallels in political and social situations.

herald: a heavenly messenger or one motivated by the LORD, whose sovereignty over Edom, and over the world, is presumed. He controls the movements and policies of *the nations*. The action against Edom is to be carried out by these nations, not by direct attack from Israel. *I heard:* prophets were inspired in different ways. The title refers to a vision which is graphically described in verses 2-4. But the actual message is perceived as something heard, not something seen. The news, or rumour, of military action being planned against Edom is confirmed.

2. The oracle is repeated in the LORD's own words to Edom. It breaks out of historical realism to picture a confrontation between God and Edom: a reminder that God's decisions control the destiny of nations. The denunciation is expressed in terms of Edom's pride being brought low. This is all the more appropriate because she had made her actual home 'on the heights'.

3. Pride is not only the sin being judged; it would also lead to Edom's fatal miscalculation. The natural fortification of her country provided a false sense of security, but she had ignored the moral laws and the higher sovereignty of God, for whom the rocky heights were no barrier. The ruins of Petra belong to a later age, but they illustrate for the modern tourist the inaccessibility of Edom's home.

4. The oracle confronts Edom with God's announcement. He says, *I will bring* her *down*. It does not matter how high her home or her walls if God is her judge.

The closing sentence marks this as a prophetic word to be received with solemn attention. God himself stands behind the message.

These verses are closely paralleled in Jer. 49: 14–16. There can be no doubt that they are only two versions of the same prophecy. It is an example of the way prophecies were remembered and used again with new application in a later age much as we use scripture for preaching and religious instruction. ✲

COMPLETE DESTRUCTION

If thieves or robbers come to you by night,   5[a]
    though your loss be heavy,
  they will steal only what they want;
  if vintagers come to you,
  will they not leave gleanings?
  But see how Esau's treasure is ransacked,   6

[a] *Verses 5 and 6: cp. Jer. 49: 9, 10.*

his secret wealth hunted out!

7 All your former allies march you to the frontier,
your confederates mislead you and bring you low,
      your own kith and kin lay a snare for your feet,
           a snare that works blindly, without wisdom.

8   And on that very day
      I will destroy all the sages of Edom
         and leave no wisdom on the mount of Esau.
      This is the very word of the LORD.

9   Then shall your warriors, O Teman, be so enfeebled,
    that every man shall be cut down on the mount of Esau.

10   For the murderous violence done to your brother
         Jacob
you shall be covered with shame and cut off for ever.

✻ A second oracle supports the first and elaborates on it. It stresses the totality of the devastation and describes the nature of the political and military crisis that Edom faces. The messengers announced in verse 1 have succeeded. Edom's allies have decided on treachery. The oracle closes with three explanations of the turn of events: the loss of wise political counsel (verse 8); the weakness of Edom's forces (verse 9); both these have been brought about by the LORD's judgement for crimes against Israel (verse 10).

5. Proverbial examples of limited loss and of harvest are given. Rarely do robbers steal everything. Traditional Near Eastern charity left some of the harvest for the poor. But neither properly describes Edom's fate.

6. By contrast, Edom's predicted disaster can only draw an exclamation of horror. An historical description of the fulfilment of this prophecy is not available. But it must have happened in much this way, since Edom disappeared entirely in the first quarter of the fifth century B.C. The destruction will be like that of a defeated city plundered by a conquering

army: everything of value will be stolen, every house and building ransacked in search of more. What the army cannot carry, it will destroy without a thought. Nothing escapes the odd mixture of wrath and glee which is so typical of such moments.

Esau is a synonym for Edom, a reminder of the ancient kinsman of Israel. The reference here prepares for the juxtaposition of Esau and Jacob in verses 9–10. The name is emotionally significant. It cannot help but remind the hearer of Jacob's successful trickery of his elder brother as he bought a birthright for a bowl of broth (Gen. 25: 27–34).

7. The way in which Edom is to be stripped of the sure defences of her mountain retreat is revealed. Her allies treacherously lure her out of her fortress. As her forces are deployed at *the frontier* in open ground, the trap is sprung. With the rocky heights stripped of defenders, a conquest will be relatively simple. The irony of Edom's fall made possible by the treachery of allies and kin is a counterpart to her crimes against Judah who, at one time, considered herself Edom's ally and kin but who was betrayed. Edom answers her allies' call with no suspicion. Her military intelligence has failed completely.

8. A hint of theological support for the prophecy breaks through in the phrase *on that very day*. The 'day of the LORD' shows the setting of the prophecy. The LORD is on his throne. He is judge over the nations. It is the day to right wrongs, to justify the innocent, and to punish the guilty.

The irony is heightened by the stupidity of Edom's manoeuvre. She was famed for her *wisdom* and cunning, her *sages* and counsel. They fail because the LORD himself has removed their balanced judgement. The action brings their destruction and ends the period of Edom's famed wisdom. The beginning of the oracle (verse 5) had shown the proverb to be inadequate to describe these events. Perhaps this inadequacy is related to the disappearance of wisdom from Edom.

The reminder that this is the LORD's word calls for solemn

heed and recognition. It would normally come at the end of the oracle (verse 10).

9. The loss of wise leadership is accompanied by the weakening of the armed forces. *Teman* is used as a synonym of the country. The disaster will depopulate the whole land, *the mount of Esau*.

No historical event has been found to fit this description. It needs none. The oracle is written as a prediction of a yet future event. The message announced in verse 1 probably named the assailants. Perhaps these were the Arabian tribes who are often credited with the final destruction of Edom. The value of the prophecy is not to be found in its historical data, but in the judgement it pronounced and the theological basis for that judgement which it proclaimed.

10. The charges against Edom close the oracle. She is accused of *murderous violence...to* her *brother Jacob*. Murder is bad enough; fratricide is a heinous crime. The decreed punishment calls for *shame* and perpetual extinction as a people. ✻

EDOM'S TREACHERY AT JERUSALEM

11   On the day when you stood aloof,
      on the day when strangers carried off his wealth,
      when foreigners trooped in by his gates
      and parcelled out Jerusalem by lot,
      you yourselves were of one mind with them.

12   Do not gloat over your brother on the day of his
         misfortune,
      nor rejoice over Judah on his day of ruin;
      do not boast on the day of distress,

13   nor enter my people's gates on the day of his downfall.
      Do not gloat over his fall on the day of his downfall
      nor seize his treasure on the day of his downfall.

14   Do not wait at the cross-roads to cut off his fugitives
      nor betray the survivors on the day of distress.

* Whatever Edom's earlier transgressions against Israel or Judah may have been, the climax was reached in her participation in the looting of Jerusalem when it fell to Nebuchadnezzar in 587 B.C. and in her refusal of asylum to King Zedekiah and his small band of refugees at that time (2 Kings 25: 3–7). The city was besieged, plundered, and systematically destroyed. When all hope was lost, the king and part of his army tried to slip through the enemy lines to safety, but were apparently caught near Jericho. These lines in Obadiah suggest that Edom was responsible for the capture.

The plundering of the city lasted a month. This may have provided time for Edom's participation. The account in 2 Kings does not suggest Edom's guilt, but Ps. 137: 7 and Lam. 4: 21–2 join Obadiah in accusing Edom.

11. Israel's sense of kinship was outraged by Edom's behaviour. It was unthinkable that she should join *strangers* and *foreigners* against her own kin. But that is exactly what she had done. Jerusalem found it hard enough to bow to the foreigner, but to have her neighbours standing by and rejoicing, even appropriating some of the booty, was just too much to bear.

12–13. Edom is chided for her malicious behaviour on the occasion: gloating, boasting, stealing *his treasure*.

14. But more serious than that was the final dastardly act of ambush laid for the fleeing king and the pitiful survivors of the siege that accompanied him. The result of that capture had been the execution of the royal princes within sight of the king, the blinding of the king, and his imprisonment in Babylon (2 Kings 25: 4–7). *

THE DAY OF THE LORD

For soon the day of the LORD will come on all the 15
    nations:
    you shall be treated as you have treated others,
    and your deeds will recoil on your own head.

16   The draught that you have drunk on my holy mountain
        all the nations shall drink continually;
            and shall drink and gulp down
            and shall be as though they had never been;

✶ During the years of exile the Jews lamented this treachery
in the bitter tones of Ps. 137 and Lam. 4. Obadiah announces
a step in the long process of restitution. A small remnant of the
people had returned in 538 B.C. A temple had been built in the
ruined city of Jerusalem. These were only tokens. But faith
recognized that God was still on his throne. He was still the
king over nature and history. The ritual of the New Year
(cp. p. 4) witnessed to this faith and was a vehicle of its
proclamation and nurture. But much remained to be fulfilled
of God's promises to Israel.

One major item of unfinished business concerned Edom.
Israel's bitterness recognized Edom's crime as one against the
LORD and his sanctuary as well as against his people. The
prophetic message now turns to this. God is giving his attention to this detail. It is only one part of God's great agenda.
But action against Edom is a sign that he has not forgotten,
and that he does work for justice in history.

15. Support for the prophecy of doom over Edom lies in
the announcement of the approach of *the day of the LORD*:
a time of judgement on *all the nations*. The indictment and
punishment of Edom is an example of what is in store for the
other peoples as well. The groups of prophecies against
foreign nations elsewhere (cp. pp. 5f.) show this to be true.
To obtain perspective the individual prophecy should be
viewed in this larger setting. Each of these prophecies ex-
pounds one text: 'the LORD comes to judge the nations'. This
includes Israel. The theme was essential and central to the faith
of Israel and to her worship in the New Year festival during
the period of the monarchy and afterwards. Belief in the
universal sovereignty of the LORD suggests that universal
scope of the judgement.

The second line enunciates the principle on which judge-ment is based. It is one of fair retribution. It can be exercised without reference to prior revelation or religious knowledge. Old Testament parallels used it regularly to make 'the punish-ment fit the crime'.

16. Judgement on Edom is pictured as a bitter cup of poison which she is forced to swallow. It is seen as a type of judgement on all nations. The same figure appears in Jer. 25: 15–29.

on my holy mountain lends the picture a perspective not yet touched. Edom's guilt came not only from a crime against her neighbour, but also from desecrating territory holy to the LORD. By doing this she had despised him and challenged his integrity.

Such rebellious folly openly flaunts the authority of the LORD. It is characteristic of the attitude of nations to the kingdom of God and constitutes a basic issue in the judgement scene. What Edom stands accused of doing is typical of all nations; Edom's punishment is equally applicable to them.

The crime punishes itself. As Edom and the nations have drunk and revelled on the mountain of the LORD's holiness, they will continue to do until they have drunk themselves into incoherent babbling and finally into the oblivion of total unconsciousness, even perhaps to a drunkard's death. This process leaves little room for formal accusation, indictment and punishment. It shows how sin inevitably brings results which are its reward. God's judgement is to be seen as much in this as in his direct punishment.

In a general way this verse repeats the judgement spoken over Edom in verses 4 and 9. *

RETURN AND RESTORATION FOR ISRAEL

but on Mount Zion there shall be those that escape,   17
  and it shall be holy,
and Jacob shall dispossess those that dispossessed them.
Then shall the house of Jacob be fire,   18

> the house of Joseph flame,
> and the house of Esau shall be chaff;
> they shall blaze through it and consume it,
> and the house of Esau shall have no survivor.
> The LORD has spoken.

19   Then they shall possess the Negeb, the mount of Esau,
> and the Shephelah of the Philistines;
> they shall possess the country-side of Ephraim and Samaria,
> and Benjamin shall possess Gilead.

20   Exiles of Israel[a] shall possess[b] Canaan as far as Zarephath,
> exiles of Jerusalem[c] shall possess the cities of the Negeb.

✻ The celebration of the LORD's dominion moved beyond judgement to portray conditions which would be made possible by his actions. He acted to halt injustice, but also to make the world conform to his will. In this the future of his own people played a central role. 'The day of the LORD' was not the end of the world, but a moment of crisis which would make things right again.

The first part of the prophecy stresses Edom's acts and God's reaction. The second in contrast describes conditions to come 'on Mount Zion'. Judgement belongs to the past.

At the time the book of Obadiah was composed Israel's exile was still a very recent memory. Israel understood it to have been God's judgement on her. This announcement of his action against Edom was a witness that the LORD was setting straight some things that had been wrong since the exile began. That the LORD was really master of the world was to be shown by the fulfilling of his promises to David con-

[a] *Prob. rdg.; Heb. adds* this army.
[b] shall possess: *prob. rdg.; Heb.* which.
[c] *Prob. rdg.; Heb. adds* who are in Sepharad.

cerning Zion. Even more was at stake in his choosing of Israel and the promise that the land of Canaan should be hers in perpetuity. Judgement against enemies like Edom would be hollow and meaningless if it did not lead to the redemption of those sacred promises by which he was known to Israel. So now the scene shifts to consider Israel's conditions and her needs.

17. In contrast to Edom's complete destruction, *Mount Zion* will be populated. God's promise to David was that a people would be there to be ruled by his dynasty for ever (2 Sam. 7).

In relation to this promise the prophets taught the doctrine of a remnant who would escape God's judgement. No matter how severe God's retaliation because of the people's corruption, some would escape to bear the blessing of David and be heirs to his promise. It may be that the idea grew out of the New Year festival (cp. p. 4 above) and that the teachings of a remnant and of the Servant of the LORD (Isa. 53) were very closely related. In their common hope for a coming anointed ruler they were both related to David. They were expressed in worship alongside prophecies against foreign nations which taught God's universal rule.

The prophecy claims the promise for a remnant on Zion and identifies the remnant as *holy*. This emphasizes its significance as a bearer of blessing and promise. The remnant is to be the prepared and purified instrument to accomplish the LORD's purpose for David, his descendants, and his kingdom. Those who had been allowed to escape and survive were to become a part of the LORD's kingdom.

The third line claims an entirely different promise: that made to Abraham and his descendants (e.g. Gen. 12: 7). This promise is symbolized in the name *Jacob*. It connects the Mosaic covenant made on Sinai to the promise that Canaan would be Israel's home. Deuteronomy is a classic expression of this faith. This line in Obadiah proclaims the reconquest of Canaan as an element of Israel's faith for the future just as Isa. 40–8 does. The translation *dispossess* follows the rendering in the Septuagint, the Greek version of the Old Testament, and in the Targum, a Jewish commentary. An alternative reading following the Hebrew is, 'possess their possession'. The Hebrew brings out the latent hope of the promise, while the versions are close parallels to verses 19–20.

18. The reference to holiness is expanded in terms of a ravaging flame. The holy remnant will be the instrument of the Holy One, i.e. God. The punishment announced in verses 4 and 9 is repeated, stressing Israel's role. Earlier in the book Israel simply heard the news or was the plaintiff seeking justice. Here she is active as the instrument of God's wrath.

The use of the names *Jacob* and *Esau* recalls the old story of rivalry between the twin brothers (Gen. 25: 27). Rather than stress the historical tensions between Judah and Edom through centuries, the prophecy uses the symbolic effect of the old story. Esau's early dominance is overcome by Jacob's persistence and patience. Jacob, not Esau, ultimately gains both land and blessing as his heritage. In this prophecy the angry reprisal Jacob had feared from Esau (Gen. 32–3) will be turned around. Israel, here described as the *house of Jacob* and *the house of Joseph*, will apply the heat of devastating wrath to Esau. Through the LORD's power it will destroy Esau totally.

The description of Edom's end in verses 4 and 9 may be historically more accurate. But the expectation that the people of God will participate in his final triumph has deep roots in Old Testament faith, although other descriptions have Israel passively witnessing the victory. The source of this may be found in the Old Testament portrayal of God's giving of Canaan to his people as the result of a 'holy war', one in which he himself engages. It may be understood as God's own battle against his opponents, or as Israel, the army of God, fighting under his command.

Again the messenger formula, *The LORD has spoken*, calls for respectful attention to the speech of God.

19. These verses make explicit the prediction that Israel would 'possess their possession' or 'dispossess those that dispossessed them' (verse 17). *they* refers to Israel, *possess* recalls

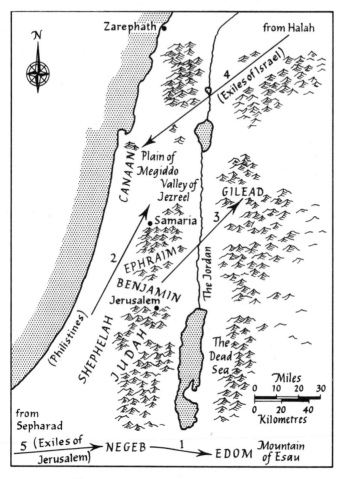

The movement of peoples in Obad. 19–20

the promise that Israel should inherit this land forever, the promise made to Abraham (e.g. Gen. 12: 7), to Israel (e.g. Exod. 3: 8) and to David (2 Sam. 7: 10). The removal of Edom will begin a series of population shifts which will rectify wrongs of the past and will fulfil God's design for his people.

The description presumes that Israelites live in Jerusalem, in the Shephelah to the west, in Benjamin immediately north of Jerusalem, and in Judah as far as the Negeb in the south. It recognizes at least two groups in distant places who would take part in the reoccupation of the land. This condition fits the situation of the Jews in the early fifth century B.C. At that time other Jews lived in Asia Minor, Egypt, North Africa and throughout Mesopotamia.

The *Negeb* lies in the south of Canaan directly west of Edom. It is a wilderness plateau area. The project of repossession will begin there when the Israelites move eastward to occupy the vacuum in Edom, the mount of Esau, after the destruction of that nation (cp. map, indicated by number 1).

The *Shephelah* is a foothill region of Judah, parallel to the Mediterranean Sea, opposite the upper part of the Dead Sea. It lies between the Philistine plain and the hill country of Judah. *Philistines* occupied this area and built important cities early in Israel's history. Their influence was permanent and the name Palestine properly identifies the area. *Ephraim* designates the ancient ancestral lands of that tribe which span the hill crest running from a point a few miles north of Jerusalem to the plain of Megiddo and the Valley of Jezreel and from the Jordan to the sea. *Samaria* is its chief city (cp. map, indicated by number 2).

The prophecy suggests a move to relieve the over-crowded condition of Judah which would bring all the expanded region under Jewish control again.

Benjamin is a narrow strip north of Jerusalem that extends eastward from the hills to the Jordan. Jews who live here will be able to expand across the Jordan to the north-east into the rich pasture and wooded land of *Gilead* (cp. map, indicated by number 3).

These shifts are reasonably clear. They provide for the expansion of the Jews into richer, better, and larger territory which formerly belonged to Israel according to the promise and providence of God.

20. This verse portrays the return of Jews from faraway places. The text is in some disorder as the notes show. *Exiles of Israel* lived in many places. A widely accepted emendation of the Hebrew for 'this army' (see N.E.B. footnote) produces the place-name 'Halah'. Halah was where exiles from the northern kingdom were sent (2 Kings 17: 6). It was located north-west of Nineveh. 'Exiles of Israel in Halah' would then parallel those 'from Jerusalem' in the next line. The promised return will include exiles from the northern tribes as well as from Judah. The return will be of 'all Israel'.

Since they are coming from the north their resettlement is logically in the area of strong Canaanite power north of Mount Carmel (cp. map, indicated by number 4). This includes the area of the Phoenician cities. *Zarephath* is a village on the coast between Tyre and Sidon where Elijah once stayed (1 Kings 17: 9–24). It is the New Testament Sarepta or Sarafand (Luke 4: 26).

The translation *shall possess* (see N.E.B. footnote) is the happy result of a slight emendation of a word which made no sense as it stood. It is the idea that dominates these verses with the fierce hope that once filled the hearts of Israel's ancestors under Joshua. Canaan was a gift from God to be possessed. The exiles longed to be back home on their own soil.

exiles of Jerusalem were those from the south. The exiles more commonly known to us were taken to the lower Mesopotamian valley by Nebuchadnezzar. But it is a mistake to assume that these were the only expatriates at this time. The Elephantine Papyri, which archaeologists discovered in Egypt and which date from the fifth century B.C., demonstrate the existence of a Jewish community in Egypt. The practice of sending men as mercenary soldiers may go back as far as Solomon's day.

The Hebrew adds 'who are in Sepharad' (see N.E.B. footnote). The location of this place has puzzled interpreters. A new suggestion identifies it as Hesperides near Benghazi on the North African coast. A garrison of Hebrew mercenaries is known to have been stationed there by the Ptolemies in the late fourth century B.C. It is possible that they were also there in the Persian period, at the time Obadiah was written. If this is the correct location, it gives the verse a particular cogency and power. As Israelite refugees return to reoccupy the northern regions of Canaan, Jewish expatriates will return from military service to reoccupy the villages of the Negeb in the south (cp. map, indicated by number 5).

Edom's disappearance would account for only the first of these population shifts. But it is seen as a sign, triggering off the series of God's acts which would fulfil the ancient promises to Israel. As he judges the nations, God is moving to accomplish his plan for Israel to be restored to her promised possession. *

DOMINION FOR THE LORD AND ZION

21   Those who find safety on Mount Zion shall go up
            to hold sway over the mount of Esau,
        and dominion shall belong to the LORD.

* The prophecy closes with this triumphant statement.

Those who find safety translates a single word which has been emended in conformity with the almost unanimous witness of the earlier versions. The Hebrew has 'saviours', in the active form. *to hold sway* translates a word usually rendered 'to judge'. Judging and saving are related terms in Old Testament usage. Hebrew judges were saviours for the people in the sense of liberating them from foreign oppression.

The faith behind the book

They were saviours for the orphan, the widow, and the oppressed. Those called to save Israel did so by exercising judgement, by creating justice. They eliminated injustice within Israel and led the people in military action against oppressors from without.

The judgements spoken in verses 4, 9, 16, and 18 are summed up. Israel will be saved by means of saviours raised up by the LORD. The ultimate objective, however, is neither the destruction of Edom nor the reconstitution of Israel. In both of these the LORD is moving to establish his dominion over all men.

The festival themes have moved full circle. They normally began with praise for God's eternal reign in heaven and his rule over nature from creation onward. They progressed to proclamation of the LORD's reign over Israel and, through her, over the world and history. Obadiah belongs to the final scene as a part of the LORD's assertion of his rule over the nations. The book weaves back and forth between the prophetic use of festal imagery (cp. p. 4 above) and historical reality to express the conviction of the LORD's ultimate complete reign. *

THE FAITH BEHIND THE BOOK

The last line of the book is the key to its meaning: 'dominion shall belong to the LORD'. Obadiah is illustrating and applying his faith in the rule of God in history. He deals only with a detail, but he presupposes the whole picture.

The LORD was known as absolute monarch over everyone in his heavenly realm. His rule in nature was established at creation and remained unchallenged. Only in the world of men has his rule been contested. The LORD wants to rule over people and nations as well as over heaven and nature. He will determine their destiny. He urges them along toward the goal he has chosen for them.

He wants justice among nations, as he seeks justice for individuals. 'As you have done, so shall it be done to you' is the principle with which justice is administered on the great day of judgement, 'the day of the LORD'. The prophet Amos had preached, almost 300 years before, that this great and terrible day would be for the nations as well as Israel.

A basic teaching of the LORD's rule on earth was that he maintained a unique relation to Israel as his own people. This doctrine was basic in the oldest interpretation of her history, probably the earliest attempt at such a history by any nation. The LORD had chosen Israel to fill a special role in his plan. This unique relation meant that he acted toward her in a different way from that toward the nations. The LORD related himself to the nations through Israel. His will for the nations was made known in Zion during Israel's festival worship.

A third doctrine determines the understanding of prophecy. It teaches that the LORD had brought Israel to Canaan and ordained that this should be her land for ever.

Obadiah apparently used the New Year's covenant festival to proclaim the doctrine of the LORD's judgement on Edom. He drew on the riches of doctrine traditionally connected with 'the day of the LORD'. The result was a work which is relevant to much more than just Edom.

The book teaches that sovereign rule belongs to the LORD. It applies that rule to one case and one time. God's rule will be realized in history. This rule applies to the affairs of states and their relations to each other. No nation is exempt. God himself demands action and accountability. Ultimately every nation and every ruler must answer to him.

The proclamation of God's dominion raises questions about his goals, his laws, and his motives. A key to his will is needed to show his purpose for the world. The key to God's work in the world is claimed to lie in his unique relation to Israel. This teaching was rooted in Israel's earliest and most basic traditions: those of Moses and Sinai in Exodus and Deuteronomy. The choosing of Israel was God's initiative to accomplish his purpose for all men. To carry out this plan, Israel was placed in the land of Canaan. The doctrine was expanded to include God's promises to David and his choice of Zion. God's relation to Israel, through Moses and David, was the prophet's key to understanding God's work in history.

The nations were judged by their relation to Israel and to Israel's king. This relation reflected their attitude toward Israel's LORD, the ruler of the whole earth. Israel was God's means of calling and testing the nations.

But there is another side to this. God protected Israel by his judgement of the nations. Israel was dependent on the LORD's strong acts to protect her borders and her people. If God did not in fact do this, it was to be understood as judgement on Israel. But her enemies were warned not to presume on such moments of judgement. God's special relation to Israel was not finally dissolved by momentary punishment. Even then God would judge the nations in terms of their attitudes towards Israel in times of her humiliation.

God's activity in the world was viewed in the Old Testament in terms of judgement and salvation. The same act might mean salvation to some and judgement to others. By its very existence Israel was an opportunity for other nations to experience the salvation or the judgement of God. In some cases, Israel was a passive spectator. In others, she, or God's anointed king in Jerusalem, was active both in judging and in making salvation possible. Obadiah presented Israel in both an active and a passive role.

These aspects of the message of Obadiah are not always seen. The book appears narrow and bigoted to the superficial reader. The reason lies in its nature as a single foreign prophecy. But if we read it in the wider context of Israel's worship and faith, then the grandeur of the Old Testament picture of God's rule over all history, portrayed in Israel, his chosen people, and in his chosen ruler, can be clearly seen. ✻

✻   ✻   ✻   ✻   ✻   ✻   ✻   ✻   ✻   ✻   ✻   ✻   ✻

JONAH

✿   ✿   ✿   ✿   ✿   ✿   ✿   ✿   ✿   ✿   ✿   ✿   ✿

A LITERARY DRAMA

This unique book is a very special piece of literature. It is a story about a prophet, but it is even more a tract about God. It uses brilliant dialogue and motifs like the fish and the gourd. Its action moves in episodes and ends with a searching question. Drama is structured like this, but there is no evidence that Jonah was ever produced on the stage. It is a narrative in dramatic form.

The book contains effective characterization. It has movement and colour. The reader identifies readily with Jonah in chs. 1 and 2. The rebuke implied in the final question strikes the reader as well as Jonah. The book uses fact and fantasy, history and art, to achieve its purpose. Its scenes are bigger than life.

God is the dominant character from beginning to end. He is Yahweh – the LORD – to Jonah as to any Israelite. Foreigners simply call him God. The prophet is the next character. The historical Jonah was an enthusiastic nationalist who predicted Israel's victories in the early eighth century (cp. 2 Kings 14: 25). In the book this tendency to narrow nationalism is stressed and satirized. Amos also criticized this kind of prophet and predicted that Assyria would come in judgement against Israel. Nineveh was Assyria's chief city. Jonah becomes a sort of anti-hero.

Foreign groups of sailors and citizens of Nineveh meet God through Jonah. They all respond to God eagerly. The wind, a fish, a gourd and a worm play important parts in the story. They are all obedient servants of God.

THEMES

The basic theme of the book is the conversion of the heathen to the worship of God and the prophet's attitude toward this. The conversion of the heathen is envisaged in Isa. 2: 2–4. It is developed in Isa. 60; Hag. 2: 6–9, and in Zech. 8: 20–3; 14: 16–21. All these derive in some measure from the promise that Abraham would become a means of blessing for all peoples (Gen. 12: 3). Jonah's theme is nearer to Jer. 18: 7–8 which proclaims the exact parallel to events which happen to Jonah in Nineveh. The beliefs of the author of Jonah are close to those of Jeremiah and the editors of the books of Kings.

A second theme is that of the reluctant or rebellious prophet. In Balaam, Elijah and Jeremiah the Old Testament sets out this theme. Elijah and Jeremiah are finally won over. The stories of Balaam and Jeremiah are told in order to preserve their prophecies. Neither of these is true for Jonah. Yet he, like them, finally performs his assigned task even if only petulantly and reluctantly.

Minor themes tell of nature's unquestioned service to the creator, of repentance and its results, of 'evil' in all its forms, and of the things men and God care about.

THE PSALM IN JONAH

The psalm in ch. 2 is very different in character and approach from the narrative. It has been inserted into the narrative by the author or a later editor. It gives a different, and deeper, perspective to the entire book. One effect of the psalm is to make the story more relevant to those who, having survived the exile, had experienced 'the depths' and had thought themselves as good as dead. Another effect of the psalm is to cast the references to life and death in ch. 4 into a different perspective. The book should be interpreted now to include the message of this psalm.

THE DATE AND AUTHOR

The book's dependence on the thoughts of Jeremiah and other writers of the seventh century is noted above. The assurance of God's care for Judah and Jerusalem given by prophets after the exile may have aroused feelings like those denounced in Jonah. Narrowly nationalistic attitudes to foreigners may be seen sometimes in Old Testament writings, particularly the oracles against the nations. It is these attitudes that are parodied in the figure of Jonah. We may distinguish this from the intense loyalty to the faith which characterizes Ezra, with his demand for strict obedience to the Law; but such loyalty may easily become narrow. No exact date can be fixed, but a time not earlier than the return from exile (537 B.C.) and not later than Ezra's reform at the end of the fifth century cannot be far wrong.

Nothing specific is known of the author. He was a highly skilled writer versed in the literature of prophecy and the Psalms. He was conversant with the ways of sailors and of the royal courts. His experiences ranged from Joppa to Nineveh. He was a man of conviction, holding fast to the best and most universal elements in Israel's religious heritage. In this book he poses questions for his generation and ours in those which are put to Jonah by the sailors and by God himself.

✫ ✫ ✫ ✫ ✫ ✫ ✫ ✫ ✫ ✫ ✫ ✫ ✫

Jonah's mission to Nineveh

ACT I – JONAH FLEES FROM GOD

Scene 1 – God's orders and Jonah's flight

THE WORD OF THE LORD came to Jonah son of 1
Amittai: 'Go to the great city of Nineveh, go now 2
and denounce it, for its wickedness stares me in the face.'
But Jonah set out for Tarshish to escape from the LORD. 3
He went down to Joppa, where he found a ship bound for
Tarshish. He paid his fare and went on board, meaning
to travel by it to Tarshish out of reach of the LORD.

✳ This scene sets the stage for the story that follows.

1. *Jonah son of Amittai* was a real prophet. The name means
'Dove, son of Truth'. His home was in Gath-hepher, 2½ miles
(4 km) north-north-east of Nazareth (2 Kings 14: 25). *came*
has the meaning of 'became reality' or 'happened to'. These
crisp words introduce a prophecy from God. The reader is
prepared to hear the voice of God speaking through his
servant.

2. The first hint that this call to prophecy is different is in
the destination given: '*Go to the great city of Nineveh.*' Other
prophets had been called to denounce a city or a people
because of their sins. It was understood, as Jonah knew well
(cp. 4: 2), that such a proclamation had a dual purpose. It
could signal the coming act of God, but it might also serve
as a last call to repentance which might turn away the coming
catastrophe (cp. Jer. 18: 7–8). Other prophets, such as Amos,
were called to prophesy about foreign countries. Some, like
Elisha, even travelled to other countries to carry out their
commissions. But no one of these had his message directed

toward a foreign people. Here an Israelite prophet, one of the chosen, is called upon to minister to a people who were not Israelite. It is inconceivable that Jonah should have refused to carry out this commission to any city or any group of Israelites. His negative reactions must be understood as conditioned by the goal of his mission. In Nineveh he could not, would not, serve.

the great city of Nineveh, which is the goal of Jonah's mission, was located on the River Tigris. In the tenth century and again from the reign of Sennacherib (about 700 B.C.) it served as the capital of the Assyrian Empire. It fell to Babylonian conquerors and was destroyed in 612 B.C. (cp. Nahum I: I). Shalmaneser I seems to have had his palace in Nineveh from 1265 to 1236 B.C. In this sense it might have been considered his capital. But Sargon II, the mightiest ruler of the eighth century, when the historical prophet Jonah lived, did not use it as his capital.

From 664 B.C., a great walled city existed on that site. Ruins have been excavated at the modern Nebi Junus, the very name of which preserves a traditional relation to Jonah. Palaces built by Sennacherib and Asshurbanipal (669–626 B.C.) have been uncovered. Both were of great size and contained valuable inscriptions. The latter left a huge library of 20,000 clay tablets which included the creation story of Enuma Elish and the Gilgamesh Epic. Worship of the goddess Ishtar dominated religious life in the city, although the corn-god Dagon was also known. The excavated walls show a city 3 miles long (nearly 5 km) and $1\frac{1}{2}$ miles (about 2 km) wide with an area of 1800 acres (about 7284 hectares). It is possible that *the great city* was intended to describe the entire complex of cities which included Calah, 18 miles (29 km) to the south, Resen, and Rehoboth-Ir. The four places appear to be collectively termed 'the great city' in Gen. 10: 12. Diodorus Siculus, writing in the first pre-Christian century, described a quadrangle 150 *stadia* by 90, or 480 in circuit (i.e. about 60 miles or 97 km). Strabo reported that it was much larger than

Babylon. It is reported that there was a period of religious reform in Assyria during the reign of Semiramis, queen regent, and her son, Adad-Nirari III (810–782 B.C.). In this reform tendencies toward monotheism may be detected similar to those of Amenophis IV in Egypt.

In the book of Jonah *Nineveh* is more than a real city. It is a symbol for all that is great and evil, all the world of people who are against God. Nineveh represents 'the nations' which God calls to world-judgement in Joel, Nahum, and other prophecies of 'the day of the LORD'.

3. In his own and God's land, where he received his commission, Jonah rises as directed, but not to go to Nineveh. He sets out for *Tarshish*. Several towns on the Mediterranean had this or a similar name. All of them were mining or smelting centres from which silver, iron, tin and lead were shipped on the largest freighters of the day which came to be called 'ships of Tarshish'. Perhaps a town in Spain is meant here, since the text implies that Tarshish was very far away (cp. Isa. 66: 19). On Jonah's map it was the extreme opposite of Nineveh, far enough even to tempt him to think he could escape from God by going there. In this way Tarshish is a symbol for the goal of all flight from God, a place *out of the reach of the LORD*.

Exactly what Jonah hoped to accomplish by his flight is not clear. It was a reaction away from all that represented this undeniable imperative of the LORD. No real Israelite thought of the presence of the LORD being limited to Canaan. Yet, under the impulse of the moment, Jonah attempted the impossible. (Cp. Isa. 49 where Israel fails to comply with God's call to service.)

The dramatic narrative is careful to show that fleeing from God degrades a person completely. Jonah goes *down* to Joppa, finds a ship going to Tarshish and goes 'down' into it (N.E.B. *went on board* does not bring this out). The next scene records his descent into the depths of the sea.

Joppa was a small harbour town on the coast of Palestine

which remained outside Israelite or Judaean control until a very late date. It is the modern Jaffa beside which the city of Tel Aviv has grown. Tyre would have been a more likely port for Jonah to go to from his home in Galilee. But a reason for the mention of Joppa may be found in the fact that it is the place where antiquity placed the story of Andromeda who was chained to a rock, threatened by a great fish, and finally rescued by Perseus or Heracles, as the various versions read. 'Jonah' is in every way different from these stories; but the association of Joppa with the stories of the 'great fish' remain.

This first scene has set the stage for the entire book. The LORD's troubles with his wilful and disobedient prophet are presented. The geographical scope of the book is shown by naming Nineveh and Tarshish. The moral horizons appear in the high call of God and the degradation implicit in Jonah's attempt to flee.

But the scene has not cited any motive for Jonah's reaction. It has not explained what God intended Jonah to do in Nineveh. *

Scene 2 – Jonah on the sea – I

4 But the LORD let loose a hurricane, and the sea ran so high in the storm that the ship threatened to break up.
5 The sailors were afraid, and each cried out to his god for help. Then they threw things overboard to lighten the ship. Jonah had gone down into a corner of the ship and
6 was lying sound asleep when the captain came upon him. 'What, sound asleep?' he said. 'Get up, and call on your god; perhaps he will spare us a thought and we shall not perish.'

* A violent storm proves false the implications of Jonah's flight: that God was powerful only in Canaan. The theme is developed through questions from the sailors and answers from Jonah.

4. The LORD's action introduces the scene. *let loose* translates a word which occurs four times to mark the actions of this scene. Its literal meaning is 'to throw'. God 'threw' the wind at the sea. The sailors threw the cargo overboard (verse 5) and later threw Jonah into the sea (verses 12, 15).

5. The anxiety of the sailors is expressed in dramatic action. In typical sailor fashion they mix curses with prayers as they throw cargo out of the ship to make it lighter. The drama is heightened as Jonah is discovered sound asleep in the hull of the ship. His slumber is rudely disturbed. If he can do nothing more for the safety of the ship, he should at least pray. A heathen captain reminds the LORD's prophet to fulfil his function as a man of God. ✳

Jonah on the sea – II

At last the sailors said to each other, 'Come and let us 7 cast lots to find out who is to blame for this bad luck.' So they cast lots, and the lot fell on Jonah. 'Now then,' 8 they said to him,*a* 'what is your business? Where do you come from? What is your country? Of what nation are you?' 'I am a Hebrew,' he answered, 'and I worship 9 the LORD the God of heaven, who made both sea and land.' At this the sailors were even more afraid. 'What 10 can you have done wrong?' they asked. They already knew that he was trying to escape from the LORD, for he had told them so. 'What shall we do with you', they 11 asked, 'to make the sea go down?' For the storm grew worse and worse. 'Take me and throw me overboard,' 12 he said, 'and the sea will go down. I know it is my fault that this great storm has struck you.' The crew rowed 13 hard to put back to land but in vain, for the sea ran higher and higher.

[a] *So Sept.; Heb. adds* who is to blame for this bad luck?

✻ 7. With Jonah once more present on deck, another episode begins. Following the common superstitions of sailors, they determine to discover *who is to blame for this bad luck*. Lots are cast and they inevitably fall upon Jonah.

8. The sailors crowd about him and ply him with every question they can think of. Under this pressure the prophet is forced to give an impromptu and unwilling testimony.

9. He confesses that *the LORD* is himself *God of heaven*, the maker of *both sea and land*. This, of course, means that he is thoroughly capable of bringing storms and of following any of his people to the ends of the earth. The storm is not 'bad luck' from an impersonal fate, but judgement from God. This confession reveals a conviction exactly opposite to the one with which Jonah apparently began to flee from the presence of God. Jonah's problem is not lack of knowledge about God. He does not agree with God, his ways, or his plans.

11. The men are appalled and ask for instructions. Throughout this scene the sailors ask the questions. Jonah's role is one of responding. He at no point takes the lead. The sailors' concern is *to make the sea go down*.

12. Again fulfilling the role of a prophet, Jonah instructs them in the ways and the will of God. The waves have been sent to catch him. If they are to stop raging, he must be given to them. *my fault* means simply 'because of me'.

13. The crew recoils from this drastic act and tries to row hard to survive the storm. But it is in vain for the *sea ran higher and higher*. ✻

Jonah on the sea – III

14 At last they called on the LORD and said, 'O LORD, do not let us perish at the price of this man's life; do not charge us with the death of an innocent man. All this, O
15 LORD, is thy set purpose.' Then they took Jonah and threw
16 him overboard, and the sea stopped raging. So the crew

were filled with the fear of the LORD and offered sacrifice and made vows to him.

✶ 14. Finally the crew give in. Jonah is offered to the waves with all the ceremony of a human sacrifice, including a prayer spoken in the name of the LORD. The prayer is a confession that the LORD is all-powerful, accustomed to do exactly as he pleases regardless of other powers or laws. The sailors do not want to protect Jonah against God's wrath at the risk of their own lives. But they also do not want to be charged with murdering Jonah. So they support their action with the plea that God's action and God's will have made it necessary.

15. They do what they feel they have to do and *threw him overboard*. And the sea immediately begins to subside. The Hebrew is not so abrupt as the translation suggests.

16. Although Jonah had grimly and stubbornly bowed to the inevitable, apparently even willing to die rather than do what God asked of him, the sailors are genuinely moved. *filled with the fear of the LORD* indicates that they had become his worshippers. They followed this with the proper acts of worship: sacrifices and vows.

The second scene shows the sovereignty of God over an area as wide as the world. He is LORD not only of Israel and of Canaan. His authority extends to the ends of the earth. There is no escape from his presence (cp. Ps. 139: 7–12).

Non-Israelites respond to God when confronted with his acts; they are converted in recognition of the LORD, sacrificing to him in continuing awe. Jonah, despite his firm intention, is forced to fill a prophetic role in identifying the LORD as the source of the storm, in interpreting what he is doing, and instructing the sailors in how they can do his will.

Jonah's illusion is ended. He cannot escape God. God demanded his life and got it. Jonah knows that he deserves this and is resigned to it. He has apparently not changed his mind. ✶

ACT II – FROM DEATH TO LIFE

Scene 1 – The great fish

17[a] But the LORD ordained that a great fish should swallow Jonah, and for three days and three nights he remained in its belly.

* 17. The LORD acts again. He is determined that the waves shall not accomplish what Jonah's flight was not allowed to do. *ordained* describes the way the LORD uses something to do his will. It is later used about the gourd vine and the worm. *a great fish* is sent to rescue God's servant. The fish, like the wind and waves, belongs to the realm of nature where the LORD's every wish is obeyed without hesitation.

This verse is the beginning of ch. 2 in the Hebrew Bible. That chapter division recognizes that it belongs more to what follows than to what has passed.

This part of the book, a very small part for it involves only three verses, uses a theme which was familiar to that part of the world. Several myths and legends told of a hero being swallowed by a sea monster. Almost all of them have some parallel to Jonah's story. The sun myth pictured the descending sun in the west as being swallowed by a monster only to reappear in the east. It was known in Persia and in Egypt. Jonah's parallel is that he travels west, is swallowed in the west, and returns in the darkness of the fish's belly to appear in the east. But if this myth had any influence on Jonah's author, he has changed it completely. Now it takes place in history, with natural creatures in the roles, and testifies to the authority of God's word and will over creation and human history.

three days and three nights: this element echoes a moon myth where three nights were reckoned as the time for the dark period of the moon. In ancient literature it also indicated a

[a] *2: 1 in Heb.*

period so long that if someone appeared to be in the realm of
death for that length of time, only divine intervention could
bring him back to life. Sometimes this realm of death was
called the grave, sometimes the underworld, or, as here, the
depths of the sea. Three days may also simply mean a fairly
long time (cp. I Sam. 30: 12; Esther 4: 16). In Jonah it
heightens the picture of the great power of God who can
save his disobedient messenger even after *three days and three
nights*. Much later Jesus' disciples on the way to Emmaus
had given up hope because 'this is the third day since it
happened' (Luke 24: 21).

Other stories have *a great fish* swallowing the hero and
spewing him out again. Even the ship's scene has a parallel
in the story of the singer Arion who was thrown overboard
by robbers only to be seen being carried away on the back of
a dolphin. But these, like the themes before, have a different
role and purpose in Jonah.

It is hardly possible that the author of Jonah was unac-
quainted with stories like these. They would have circulated
freely in cities like Joppa where some of them were supposed
to have taken place. His knowledge of sea travel could well
have come from Joppa, too. The Old Testament gives little
evidence otherwise of sea-faring ways. Exceptions are Ps.
107: 23–30 and Ezek. 27. The latter text (verses 25–8) has
exactly the same phrases as the first chapter of Jonah. But the
author could hardly have his entire inspiration from there,
else he would have chosen Tyre, not Joppa, for Jonah's trip.

The author has dealt with all these themes in a very independent fashion. He has used them at least as freely and artistically
as he has used elements from Israel's own traditions. ✶

Scene 2 – Jonah's prayer

2 Jonah prayed to the LORD his God from the belly of the
fish:

2   I called to the LORD in my distress,
       and he answered me;
     out of the belly of Sheol I cried for help,
       and thou hast heard my cry.

3   Thou didst cast me into the depths, far out at sea,
       and the flood closed round me;
all thy waves, all thy billows, passed over me.

4   I thought I was banished from thy sight
and should never see thy holy temple again.

5   The water about me rose up to my neck;
       the ocean was closing over me.
     Weeds twined about my head

6   in the troughs of the mountains;
       I was sinking into a world
     whose bars would hold me fast for ever.
     But thou didst bring me up alive from the pit, O LORD
       my God.

7   As my senses failed me I remembered the LORD,
and my prayer reached thee in thy holy temple.

8   Men who worship false gods may abandon their loyalty,

9   but I will offer thee sacrifice with words of praise;
I will pay my vows; victory is the LORD's.

   ✳ 1. This verse connects the psalm to the preceding story.
prayed is a formal word while the narrative in 1: 14 and 3: 8
simply says, 'called on God'. The more formal term is
justified, for what follows is a prayer psalm which thanks God
for salvation. *the LORD his God:* the words contrast sharply

with Jonah's disobedience and flight from God. They imply
a recognition of the worshipper's commitment to God and a
claim on God's relation to him in covenant. They suit the tone
of the psalm that follows. *from the belly of the fish:* as the first
words of this sentence do not fit the narrative that precedes it,
so this is not in line with the psalm's implication that it is a
prayer normally offered in the temple (cp. verses 4 and 9).

In this monologue Jonah looks back on the terror of the
waves and speaks to God in thanksgiving for the salvation
afforded him. The psalm is of a type familiar in the Psalter,
including motifs which occur there repeatedly. They are
right for Jonah's situation. Yet they certainly would not have
been construed by a knowing Israelite to have been composed
on the spot. The author quotes appropriate Psalm fragments.

The themes in the psalm which Jonah prays from *the belly
of the fish* have different perspectives from those of the two
scenes in Act I. The first scene dealt with the call of God and the
prophet's flight from that call, and the second presented God's
action to ensure that the prophet did not succeed in his flight.
This act speaks of destiny at its greatest possible dimension.
The issues here are life and death. Jonah describes his experience
of drowning as being separated from God. Picture after
picture portrays this experience of the abyss and of the salvation which God sent to restore him to life. The dimension
achieved in this interlude is that of a reality as big as the
universe, which deals with the final question of human existence. Here, too, God is sovereign. Jonah has learned the
meaning of that sovereignty through his own salvation.

As the prophet in ch. 1 is reminiscent of Israel to whom the
LORD had assigned a role in the salvation of the nations, so the
prophet in the fish's belly is reminiscent of Israel in exile. The
exile was God's way of saving them from the destruction of
Jerusalem. Through the exile they could face a return to
Canaan as though they had been raised from a sure death to a
surprising new life. Jonah, whom the fish has 'spewed...out
on to the dry land' (verse 10), is like the returned community

which could look back not only on the original salvation from Egypt and the covenant on Sinai which constituted Israel as God's people, but also on the release from exile which had added a new perspective to the meaning of their existence. Jonah has to look at life now, not only as a prophet who has heard the call of God, but also as one who has been undeservedly saved from the depths of the sea by God's purposeful intervention.

2–9. There is no progression in the psalm. The same experience is depicted in four cycles: verses 2, 3–4, 5–6, and 7. In each of the four a particular problem is pictured. The *distress* is related to water or the sea. But it also includes being in the *belly of Sheol, banished from* God's *sight*, and *sinking into* another *world* permanently. These are all pictures of death, as is the phrase *my senses failed me*. The psalmist's actions consist in calls to the LORD, cries for help, looking to his holy temple, remembering the LORD, and prayer to him. To these the LORD answers, heeding his voice, bringing him up alive from the pit, and allowing his prayers to come up to him.

The final strophe (verses 8–9) announces that the worshipper will fulfil his vows and bring *sacrifice with words of praise*. The psalm ends with the confession: *victory* (or salvation) *is the LORD's*. This summarizes the content of the psalm and the experience of Jonah in ch. 1. Note the similar ending of Obadiah: 'and dominion shall belong to the LORD'.

The psalm has been called a 'king's passion psalm' and related to the throwing of Jonah into the sea understood as a sacrifice which just preceded it in the story. So it has been interpreted as a typical expression of the New Year's cult (cp. p. 4). The evidence for this is far from clear. But there is no doubt that the insertion of this psalm has added another perspective to the book and its meaning. It stresses God's rescue of Jonah from death to life, from the sea to the dry land. Jewish and Christian symbolism has seized on this as a sign of resurrection.

Because of this psalm 'the sign of Jonah', which otherwise

could be restricted to the recognition of the effectiveness of
Jesus' preaching (Matt. 16: 4; Luke 11: 32), is deepened to
symbolize his resurrection (Matt. 12: 39–40). In Jewish and
Christian interpretation, the royal messianic nature of the
psalm has been recognized. The psalm changes a story, which
dealt simply with God's rescue of his prophet in order for
him to perform a task, into a drama of death's short victory
followed by resurrection to a new life of prophetic service. ✱

Scene 3 – Back on dry land

Then the LORD spoke to the fish and it spewed Jonah 10
out on to the dry land.

✱ For the third time the LORD acts to bring back his fleeing
prophet. He had 'let loose a hurricane' and had 'ordained
that a great fish should swallow Jonah'. This time he simply
spoke to the fish. In response to God's command, the fish
spewed Jonah out. *the dry land* is the opposite of the watery sea.
The psalm thought of Jonah's being swallowed by the fish as
God's act of salvation; and so it was, for it kept him from
drowning and preserved him alive through a time much
longer than one can otherwise survive in the sea. But in the
view of the story, the act of saving Jonah is completed in
getting him back to his natural habitat, the dry land. ✱

ACT III – JONAH IN NINEVEH

Scene 1 – Jonah obeys a second call

The word of the LORD came to Jonah a second time: **3**
'Go to the great city of Nineveh, go now and denounce 2
it in the words I give you.' Jonah obeyed at once and 3*a*
went to Nineveh.

✻ 1. *a second time:* these words remind the reader of the first scene. Most of this scene is an exact parallel to the first.

2. Instead of the reference to Nineveh's evil of 1: 2, the second command simply defines his message: *in the words I give you.* The most typical form of prophetic speech is one introduced by the formula a messenger would use. This verse fits that understanding of the prophetic task.

3. This time *Jonah obeyed at once and went.* He reacts in the way a prophet would be expected to react. ✻

Scene 2 – Jonah's preaching and the Ninevites' repentance – I

3*b*–4 He began by going a day's journey into the city, a vast city, three days' journey across, and then proclaimed: 'In forty days Nineveh shall be overthrown!'

✻ This first episode records Jonah's preaching. It notes that Nineveh was *a vast city, three days' journey across.* For the reader to check the actual size of the city is beside the point. The author wants to emphasize the huge size of a city many times larger than any in Palestine. The Hebrew uses the expression 'great to God' meaning that Nineveh was very large not only to a Palestinian countryman, but even in God's eyes. Jonah penetrates approximately a third of the way across the city and begins announcing the terse message which had been entrusted to him.

He utters a brief and dire prediction. The message carries no qualification, no call to repentance. '*In forty days Nineveh shall be overthrown!' forty days* is used in the Bible for times of special retreat or fasting: Moses on Sinai (Exod. 24: 18), Elijah at the same place (1 Kings 19: 8), and Jesus in the wilderness (Mark 1: 13). It denotes a full period of time. It provided time for Nineveh to react and repent.

Neither warmth nor pleading is in the message as the prophet proclaims the destruction of the city. ✻

Jonah's preaching and the Ninevites' repentance – II

The people of Nineveh believed God's word. They 5
ordered a public fast and put on sackcloth, high and low
alike. When the news reached the king of Nineveh he 6
rose from his throne, stripped off his robes of state, put
on sackcloth and sat in ashes. Then he had a proclamation 7
made in Nineveh: 'This is a decree of the king and his
nobles. No man or beast, herd or flock, is to taste food, to
graze or to drink water. They are to clothe themselves in 8
sackcloth and call on God with all their might. Let every
man abandon his wicked ways and his habitual violence.
It may be that God will repent and turn away from his 9
anger: and so we shall not perish.'

* *The people of Nineveh* react to the gloomy speech of the
reluctant prophet. They receive it as the word of God, believe
its import, and draw conclusions of what is required of them.
As one man, they repent and express their grief in forms which
are as graphic as they are sincere.

6. The king's response is typical of the people. In self-
abasement and humility before God he puts on *sackcloth*
(burlap) and sits *in ashes*. These are mourning customs suitable
for ritual repentance.

7. The royal decree proclaims a total fast. Even animals are
included. They are to eat no food, drink no water.

8. Mourning and fasting provide the setting for an urgent
appeal for God's mercy to reverse the judgement. Beyond
this, the king decrees a reversal of life pattern from *wicked
ways* to good, from *violence* to peace. Apparently the entire
people share the king's sense of urgency and agree with the
measures.

9. They have no assurance of God's response. But on the
bare possibility that God will honour their change of heart

and alter his determined will, they launch their fast, their grief, and their petition. Their response is all the more remarkable since the prophet had neither named the deity whose wrath he voiced nor stated conditions for response. The book is careful in using the words for God. The heathen speak only in the generic term, God, and do not use 'the LORD' which would name the God of Israel. They, different from the sailors, never knew it was 'the LORD' of Israel who threatened the city. ✻

Jonah's preaching and the Ninevites' repentance – III

10 God saw what they did, and how they abandoned their wicked ways, and he repented and did not bring upon them the disaster he had threatened.

✻ This time it is God who reacts. He is sensitive to the happenings in the city. Nineveh changes the life-style which had called for judgement. So God, acting in the way that is only and truly God's way, responds to their repentance and their pleas for reprieve. *he repented:* God changed his decision. It does not mean that he was sorry for wrong. As the people turn from wickedness to being open to God, he turns from wrath to mercy. The *disaster* is averted. This is exactly what Joel announced to Jerusalem (2: 12–13). Jonah had to learn that God reacts to the repentance of other nations with equal mercy.

The story does not tell how God's change of mind was revealed to Nineveh. Certainly it did not come through Jonah. But in some way the change became known to the people and to Jonah. Further proclamation of the dark prophecy was neither possible nor required. ✻

Scene 3 – Jonah's angry response

Jonah was greatly displeased and angry, and he prayed **4** 1, 2
to the LORD: 'This, O LORD, is what I feared when I was
in my own country, and to forestall it I tried to escape to
Tarshish; I knew that thou art "a god gracious and compassionate, long-suffering and ever constant, and always
willing to repent of the disaster".[a] And now, LORD, take 3
my life: I should be better dead than alive.' 'Are you so 4
angry?' said the LORD.

✣ 1. *greatly displeased* is literally 'it became evil to Jonah as a
great evil' playing on the word which appears so often in the
book. God's mercy on Nineveh is 'an evil' to Jonah. His
reaction to the change is instantaneous and passionate. He
feels betrayed. His hurt feelings feed the fires of bigoted
shock. He turns his fury on God.

2. *prayed:* exactly the same word used in 2: 1 but with a
very different content. This prayer is neither formal nor
correct. But it does represent a complaint against God which
is the technical meaning of the term. Now Jonah thinks he
can justify himself for having tried to prevent this 'shameful'
turn of events by avoiding God's call in the first place. He
says he knew something like this would happen.

I knew: the prophets repeatedly state the goal of revelation
to be 'that you may know'. Jonah's knowledge was accurate.
He knew what God was like, but he did not agree with him.
This is the basic sin of man. The prophets often speak of it as
rebellion. In citing the correct theology which he rejected,
Jonah quotes Exod. 34: 6. This verse had a remarkable
influence in the Old Testament (cp. Joel 2: 13; Num. 14: 18;
Pss. 86: 15; 103: 8; 145: 8; Nahum 1: 3; Neh. 9: 17). The
relation of Jonah to Joel is particularly close here because they
alone have *gracious* first followed by *compassionate*. This is the

[a] a god…disaster: *cp. Exod. 34: 6.*

reverse order of all the other references. But a more important connection is that only these two add: *and always willing to repent of the disaster.* The verse would be pertinent any time a disastrous judgement has been announced and God's forgiveness is being sought. But these two books go beyond the Exodus verse in that God 'repents' of the threat (cp. Jer. 18: 7–8).

Jonah contends that he had refused to go on this mission because he did not agree with God's policies, although he knew exactly what they were. In saying this Jonah posed a basic theological problem: the tension between belief in a God of justice and a God of grace. Jonah did not want a God of grace, at least not for Nineveh. In quoting Exod. 34: 6 Jonah confessed that Israel owed its existence to the mercy and compassion of God, to his willingness to forgive the penitent, even to his patience with the impenitent. Jonah himself, no less than the people, owed his life to God's grace and long-suffering.

Whatever Jonah's original motives may have been in fleeing from God's call, he here tries to give them theological respectability. He is shocked at God's willingness to respond to a heathen people's sincere repentance. Jonah implies a lack of determination and consistency in God's actions. With a hint of superiority Jonah lectures God for his weakness and softness in relation to Nineveh.

3. In his passion Jonah pleads for the privilege of death. He seems to say that he would rather not continue to live in a world that has a gracious God. He feels betrayed. God's change of heart casts doubt on Jonah's accuracy as a prophet. But other prophets, like Amos, Zephaniah, and Joel, pleaded with people to repent in the hope that the announcements they had just made would not have to be fulfilled. Elijah had also asked to die (1 Kings 19: 4) in a scene that may have been a model for this passage. But Elijah did so in view of the apparent victory of the heathen forces of Jezebel over God's people.

If the book of Jonah once existed without the psalm in ch. 2, this request to die would be shocking enough. But with the psalm's presentation of the awfulness of death and the wonder of life from God, Jonah's preference for death, and all it represented, to continuing to live in a world in which God's grace extends even to heathen people in Nineveh is almost unbelievable.

4. God's answer neither derides nor despises Jonah. But his question penetrates the façade of righteous anger. *Are you so angry?* is literally, 'Is it good for you to be angry?' or, 'Does it do any good – this anger (or evil) of yours?' In view of Nineveh's repentance and God's grace, is it fitting for the prophet of God to be so angry, so petulant, so opposed to the mercy of God?

Throughout ch. 4 God acts, Jonah reacts, and God asks Jonah questions which get no answers. In ch. 1 the sailors asked the questions, but there Jonah was forced to give answers. Here the questions go unanswered, for the nature of the book is to pose questions for its readers rather than to lecture to them.

This act is the longest and in many ways the greatest in the book. It begins with Jonah's preaching in Nineveh, continues with the wide-spread and complete repentance of the Ninevites and the signs of God's having repented of his judgement on Nineveh, and ends with this exchange between Jonah and God concerning Nineveh. God's compassion for the Ninevites is plain. He is shown to be prepared to exercise mercy and understanding when they seek it.

Yet Jonah's unwillingness to accept God's mercy for the heathen is equally plain and the heat of his anger almost burns the pages. The anger displayed in this scene is a majestic, even heroic anger. Jonah appears to be a great man, whether in flight or in anger, one willing to argue with God to maintain his view of what is right. The first hint of a turn in the drama comes in the patient yet probing tones of God's question – a question which Jonah never seems to have asked: are his anger and conviction justified? ✳

ACT IV – JONAH'S CARES AND THE LORD'S CARE – I

5 Jonah went out and sat down on the east of the city. There he made himself a shelter and sat in its shade, 6 waiting to see what would happen in the city. Then the LORD God ordained that a climbing gourd[a] should grow up over his head to throw its shade over him and relieve his distress, and Jonah was grateful for the gourd.

✻ 5. Jonah, no longer in Nineveh, *sat down on the east of the city* presumably to wait out the forty days to see whether his prophecy might even yet be fulfilled. He prepares for his vigil by making *himself a shelter*. This was probably a fragile booth with branches of palms or trees thrown over it. No one in the east would sit directly in the sun.

6. *the LORD God:* the names for God have been chosen very carefully throughout the book. This double name combines the covenant name *the LORD* with the general word which the Ninevites and everyone else would recognize. The LORD of Israel is also the God of all the world. *ordained:* the word portrays God's use of something for his special purpose. It appeared in 1: 17 for the great fish and will also be used in 4: 7–8 for the worm and the wind.

a climbing gourd: some translators and commentators from an early date have identified the plant as a castor-oil plant (cp. N.E.B. note). Jonah already had some shade, but the living plant made it denser and more refreshing. The purpose is to *relieve* him from *his distress*. The Hebrew word here is 'evil' which is used so often. It means his bad mood.

grateful is much too mild for the Hebrew, 'rejoiced with a great joy'. The very bad mood turned into a very good mood just because of the green protection from the sun. ✻

[a] a climbing gourd: *or* a castor-oil plant.

JONAH'S CARES AND THE LORD'S CARE – II

But at dawn the next day God ordained that a worm 7
should attack the gourd, and it withered; and at sunrise 8
God ordained that a scorching wind should blow up
from the east. The sun beat down on Jonah's head till he
grew faint. Then he prayed for death and said, 'I should
be better dead than alive.' At this God said to Jonah, 'Are 9
you so angry over the gourd?' 'Yes,' he answered,
'mortally angry.' The LORD said, 'You are sorry for the 10
gourd, though you did not have the trouble of growing
it, a plant which came up in a night and withered in a
night. And should not I be sorry for the great city of 11
Nineveh, with its hundred and twenty thousand who
cannot tell their right hand from their left, and cattle
without number?'

✴ 7. The action begins *at dawn*, presumably while Jonah
sleeps, secure in his new comfort. God *ordained that a worm
should attack the gourd, and it withered*. The source of Jonah's
great joy grew in a few hours and withered in as many
minutes.

8. The next action occurs *at sunrise*. Even before the heat
of the day, a *scorching wind* from *the east* brought the desert
heat and apparently blew away even the shelter of the booth
which Jonah had built for himself. The direct rays of the sun
beat down on Jonah's head. It is no surprise that without shelter
Jonah *grew faint*. His mood turns to despair. *he prayed for death*
using exactly the same words that he had used in his anger
over the forgiveness of Nineveh.

9. God's question is also the same as in verse 4 with the
addition of *over the gourd*. In the temper of the moment Jonah
replies, '*Yes, mortally angry.*'

In this setting outside the city Jonah is no longer the heroic figure opposing God in what he considers to be a righteous cause. The mercurial rise and fall of his disposition has demonstrated how unstable he is. His protest of mortal anger evokes a pitying laugh instead of serious acceptance. All he has said and done is seen as the work of an immature person, speaking and acting in the heat of emotional complexes. His talk of death is like that of a child who knows neither the meaning of life nor the cost of death. He is in no way fit to speak for God, much less to pass judgement on him.

10. The LORD sums up Jonah's reactions. *sorry for* is a synonym for 'repented' of 3: 10. It can also mean 'pity' or 'care about'. Jonah cared so much for trivial things. The passing and momentary significance of the vine is stressed: it *came up in a night and withered in a night*.

11. The supreme question of the book is: *should not I be sorry?* The good news of the Bible is that God does care, even if pragmatic men can never understand why. *the great city of Nineveh* is contrasted to the gourd vine. The size is given in huge numbers. They are not intended to be exact, but to impress. *who cannot tell their right hand from their left:* these could be small children; but the words could equally well be used for the mass of poor and illiterate people who live out their lives with no chance to make the decisions that will determine their fate. *and cattle:* God's concern reaches beyond the people to the animals who are a part of every such eastern city even today. In contrast to Jonah's gourd which he had neither planted nor laboured to cultivate, God's concern is for creatures that he created, for persons that he wanted to become his own people.

The basic message of this last chapter is a plea for God's right to care for the important things of the world, for great cities where uncounted people stir in their ignorance before an uncertain fate. It implies a judgement on man's petty concerns and an invitation to share God's larger concern.

The psalm in this book has caught the attention of Jews and Christians. Jewish writings and early art picture Jonah as a symbol of the resurrection, while Christian portrayals in church art have made him the greatest of the prophets, the one next to Christ. This need not distract the modern reader from the basic question of the book. It should only intensify it. God claims a right to care about the masses of humanity. He extends this claim through the Christian and the Church, just as surely as he does through the Jew and the Synagogue. *

*   *   *   *   *   *   *   *   *   *   *   *   *

NAHUM

✳   ✳   ✳   ✳   ✳   ✳   ✳   ✳   ✳   ✳   ✳   ✳   ✳

1 An oracle about Nineveh: the book of the vision of Nahum the Elkoshite.

✳ The title is in two parts. The first is very closely related to the contents and would have been read aloud with the following material. *oracle* is sometimes translated 'burden' and is thought to have implied a message of doom. However, it became a technical term for a prophecy spoken against a nation under judgement.

Nineveh: the book is about the coming destruction of this city. Its name is important in the title since the city is not mentioned in the book until 2: 8. Only by naming it in the title can hearers be aware of what the following verses are about. The book of Jonah is also concerned with Nineveh (cp. Jonah 3: 2–3). Jonah was written at least a century and a half later and looked back on the great city that was. Nahum deals with a city that still exists, though now past its prime. Nineveh was the most important city of the Assyrian Empire (cp. Gen. 10: 11–12). It was built on the banks of the River Tigris about 5000 B.C. It had its share in the rising power of Assyria early in the second millennium B.C. but its greatest period came during the last century of the empire (730–612 B.C.).

The buildings of that period are associated with the great emperors Sennacherib, Esarhaddon and Asshurbanipal. The city was heavily fortified behind two sets of walls. Great palaces and temples were built. Ishtar, goddess of love and war, ruled supreme and was appropriately recognized. The finest gate was dedicated to her and decorated with her image and symbols. Rich monuments and friezes recorded both the artistry and wealth of the period. One palace has been found to contain the best library in the world of that time, filled with books inscribed on clay tablets. Streets and gardens were built to an extent unknown in the ancient world.

Assyrian power was first felt in the Mesopotamian valley where it inherited the crumbling Hittite and Mitanni empires. Not until the eighth century did Assyrian rulers look westward toward the Mediterranean Sea. Just after the middle of that century Sargon II and later Sennacherib sent their armies into Aram, then down into Judah, and finally as far as Egypt. Some of the earliest of recorded prophecies note these movements and interpret them as God's dealing with Israel and the nations. Amos (3: 9) summoned Assyria and Egypt, the great powers of his day, to witness the corruption of Samaria, while his description in 6: 1–2 refers to Assyrian victories by Tiglath-pileser III. Isaiah warned Ahaz in Jerusalem that Assyria was the nation to fear. He prophesied that the coming of the Assyrians was actually the intention and the work of God (10: 5–16).

Samaria fell to the Assyrians in 721 B.C. (2 Kings 17). Judah, like the surrounding countries, was a vassal to Assyria during most of the following century. The vassalage was enforced by the power of Assyrian arms on several occasions, most conspicuously in the siege of Jerusalem in 701 B.C. (2 Kings 18). Assyria's power began to wane in the last quarter of the seventh century (cp. the introduction, p. 9). Josiah apparently owed his relative freedom of action for reform to this fact.

As part of the crumbling Assyrian power, Nineveh fell to Babylonian and Median attack in the summer of 612 B.C. Nahum must have composed his prophecy near this time. Some interpreters think it was written after the event and that it is a celebration of the fall. However, the book's prophetic and visionary character suggest that it was written shortly before the fall. The prophets often present their pictures of the future as though they had already happened. This seems to be the case in 2: 11–12 and 3: 18–19.

The last of the great Assyrian emperors died about 626 B.C. This opened the door to the reforms of Josiah in Judah. The final chapter of Assyria's history began in 614 B.C. when her enemies allied themselves against her. Nahum's work served as an interpretation of these events. He predicted that they would be successful. The repetition of his powerful prophetic poems became a kind of prayer that Assyria's power would be broken. In this he undoubtedly knew of Isaiah's earlier prediction of the limits of God's toleration of Assyrian power (Isa. 10: 12f.).

Nahum's work must have been spoken or read before an assembly in the temple. After Nineveh's fall it continued to be used as a witness to fulfilled prophecy and to God's action. By this means it found its way into the collection of the twelve prophets and the Old Testament canon.

The second part of the title belongs to the written record. Nahum is the only prophetic work to be called a *book*. The word can refer to a written text of any size. Its original use was more like that of a sermon text intended to be preached, or a play script which is intended to be spoken. Temple services afforded occasions for it to be read pertinently, and it may be that this reading accompanied dramatic action which made its sudden changes of address have meaning.

The writing records a *vision*. This inspired experience of God's message is a form frequently related to prophecy. In a vision the usual restrictions of reason, time and space recede and the prophet is seized by a compulsion to see and speak in a heightened consciousness that he recognizes to be from God. The excellent poetic form of the book was understood to be a direct result of such 'inspiration'.

Nahum is a name not otherwise known in the Old Testament. It means 'comfort'. If the name was given by his father, it confessed a faith in God's comfort for his people. *the Elkoshite* means he was from Elkosh, an unidentified place only mentioned here.

No information about the prophet or his life is given. He must have been one of the prophets closely associated with the temple in Jerusalem. His work shows a familiarity with prophetic traditions and with temple rituals. His concern for international relations is appropriate for Jerusalem as the capital. He fulfilled the highest calling of prophecy in looking beyond the 'facts' of the news to discern and proclaim the intentions of God.

The first parts of the book of Nahum set the stage for his tremendous pictures of the fall of Nineveh. A poem describes the vengeance God takes on his enemies (verses 2–8). It is followed by a section addressing the enemies (verses 9–11) and a section of hope for Israel (1: 13 – 2: 2). ✶

The vengeance of the LORD
on his enemies

The LORD is a jealous god, a god of vengeance;   2[a]
the LORD takes vengeance and is quick to anger.[b]
[c]In whirlwind and storm he goes on his way,   3
    and the clouds are the dust beneath his feet.
He rebukes the sea and dries it up   4
    and makes all the streams fail.
Bashan and Carmel languish,

[a] *Verses 2–14 are an incomplete alphabetic acrostic poem; some parts have been re-arranged accordingly.*
[b] *The rest of verse 2*, The LORD takes...wrath, *transposed to verse 11.*
[c] *Prob. rdg.; Heb. inserts two lines* The LORD is long-suffering and of great might, but the LORD does not sweep clean away.

and on Lebanon the young shoots wither.

5   The mountains quake before him,
　　　the hills heave and swell,
　and the earth, the world and all that lives in it,
　　　are in tumult at his presence.

6   Who can stand before his wrath?
　　　Who can resist his fury?
　His anger pours out[a] like a stream of fire,
　and the rocks melt[b] before him.

7   The LORD is a sure refuge
　for those who look to him[c] in time of distress;
　he cares for all who seek his protection

8   and brings them safely[d] through the sweeping flood;
　he makes a final end of all who oppose him
　and pursues his enemies into darkness.

9–11   No adversaries dare oppose him twice;
　all are burnt up[e] like tangled briars.
　Why do you make plots against the LORD?
　He himself will make an end of you all.
　From you has come forth a wicked counsellor,
　plotting evil against the LORD.
　The LORD takes vengeance on his adversaries,
　against his enemies he directs his wrath;
　with skin scorched black, they are consumed
　like stubble that is parched and dry.

[a] pours out: *or* fuses *or* melts.
[b] *Prob. rdg.; Heb.* are torn down.
[c] for…him: *prob. rdg., cp. Sept.; Heb. om.*
[d] brings them safely: *prob. rdg.; Heb. om.*
[e] all are burnt up: *prob. rdg.; Heb.* for until.

✻ The opening verses are an acrostic poem – each strophe of two lines beginning with succeeding letters of the Hebrew alphabet. The N.E.B. footnote suggests that this extends to verse 14, which is possible but uncertain, for the alphabetic structure is in fact only clear as far as verse 8. The change of theme in verses 9–11 fits with this, but there is no certainty in the matter, partly because of the many problems of inter-pretation. In Jerusalem the LORD was worshipped as the one who sustained and protected all life and institutions for his people. His rule included the entire universe. He was the giver of life, the upholder of order, throughout the world. He would conquer and eliminate all that was harmful or disruptive in his universal kingdom.

2. This poem and those that follow fit that concept. They picture God's movement to overcome the powers of evil. His determination and zeal to accomplish this are pictured in the term *a jealous god* (cp. comments on Joel 2: 18 and 27). The same description supports the command against making images (Exod. 20: 5; 34: 14). It means that God will not tolerate opposition or a frustration of his plans. He is 'pas-sionately determined' that his rule will be accepted throughout his realm. His victory will be for the benefit of his trusting people. *a god of vengeance:* the vengeance of God is on behalf of the afflicted. It sets the balance of justice straight again. God does not overlook the wrongs done. *quick to anger* is literally 'owner' or 'master' of anger. It pictures his capacity to carry out his vengeance.

After these first two lines the Hebrew text has two strophes which have apparently been inserted into the text breaking the order of alphabetical lines. The one in verse 2 has been moved in the N.E.B. to verse 11 (cp. footnote). The second is in verse 3 (cp. footnote) and has been omitted in the trans-lation. The added text assures readers who question why God's vengeance is not already apparent that God has his own time-table for justice. 'long-suffering' is a reference to Exod. 34: 6, but is applied here in a very different context. 'of great might' asserts that there is no lack of power to effect justice. 'does not sweep clean away' means that he will not overlook evil. The R.S.V. is perhaps clearer here: 'will by no means clear the guilty'.

3. Two strophes announce the LORD's actions against the seas. *whirlwind and storm* are frequent symbols of God's presence in the Old Testament. He is so high that *the clouds are his roads*.

4. *the sea* was a symbol in Near Eastern mythology and in Old Testament poetry for the powers of evil and chaos. Whatever powers for destruction it may have, God's action and word are sufficient to reduce it to impotence. God's control of the water sometimes means that he uses it for judgement by bringing drought. *Bashan* is a plateau area east of the Sea of Galilee which was one of the most fertile areas in Palestine. *Carmel* is a mountain that thrusts out to the very edge of the Mediterranean just below modern Haifa. It was normally well-watered and green. *Lebanon* was also known for its great trees and green mountain slopes. But all of these are hurt by the LORD's rebuke of the sea and the streams.

5. The great powers of the earth are in utter confusion in the presence of the LORD: *mountains*, *hills*, *the earth*, *the world*.

6. The description of God's approach draws on the figures of the great creation drama in which God makes an ordered universe by overcoming all hostile powers. His victories lead to the anguished question: *Who can stand before his wrath?* No one can stand up to such a *stream of fire* which melts even the rocks (cp. Ps. 97: 1–5). Nahum thinks God's action against Nineveh will be like his victory over all opposition to establish the universe. No power in heaven or on earth can oppose him successfully.

7. But there is another side to God's action. *a sure refuge* is literally 'the LORD is good to be a refuge in the day of wrath'. Not only jealous, but good. The division runs through the world between those who oppose him and those *who look*

to him and *who seek his protection*. His power for the latter means security and assurance (cp. Ps. 91).

8. But the former are destined for a *final end*. The Hebrew verse division has *the sweeping flood* related to the destruction of enemies which follows. The great waters are now seen as God's instrument rather than his enemy. *all who oppose him* stands in place of Hebrew words which apparently mean 'her place'. 'By the sweeping flood he will make an end of her place.' This is the first reference to one of God's enemies as feminine, although there will be others in the following verses; for example, in 2: 5–7 where 'her' palace is carried away by the waters and 'she' is captured.

This feminine pronoun may stand for Nineveh. But it also may point to her patron goddess, Ishtar, and even beyond Ishtar to the creator's great enemy who represents chaos in the creation epic (cp. Isa. 51: 9–11). God's vengeance promises an end to 'the enemy' whether on the level of history (Nineveh) or on that above history (Ishtar, chaos). Those who stand with her as demonic allies are also God's *enemies*. One of these will be mentioned in 1: 11 and 15. They are to be *pursued into darkness*. This is the darkness of the underworld, the world of death and demons where they belong.

9–11. This passage is linked to the preceding poem through the idea that the LORD will 'make a final end' (verse 8) which is repeated literally in the Hebrew although it is omitted in the translation. It differs from the poem in using direct address. What is not always clear is who is being addressed. If this was first presented in a kind of liturgy, different speakers and dramatic action would have made this much easier to follow than it is when one only reads the text.

oppose him twice translates a Hebrew verb which can also be 'she shall not stand up to his anger twice'. The use of the feminine in verse 8 for 'her place' has already been noted. The intention is not to make a general statement about the LORD's prowess (as the N.E.B. translation seems to imply) but to assert that the LORD's action against Nineveh and her patroness will be so devastating that no second battle will be possible. This is an explanation of 'he makes a final end' (verse 8).

tangled briars are those that have been cut and dried out. They are therefore highly combustible.

Why do you make plots? the address is masculine plural and must refer to the leaders of Nineveh or her military officers. Behind them stand the votaries of Ishtar. In a contest with the LORD they will be a part of the *end* which is sure for their patroness. *From you* must have a feminine singular antecedent. This is surely Nineveh/Ishtar. *counsellor* is a courier or messenger. *wicked* translates the Hebrew word 'belial' which has often been understood as meaning 'worthless'. However, there is also a good possibility that it is a proper name for a demon or a devil meaning 'swallower' (cp. comment on I Sam. I: 16 in this series). Recent interpretations have taken it in this way. Belial is then a demonic representative of Ishtar/Nineveh *plotting evil against the LORD*. This is what King Sennacherib did when he came from Nineveh to curse the LORD at Jerusalem (2 Kings 18–19). But the conflict between the LORD and his enemies is also seen at the level of God's great war on cosmic and supernatural evil. Belial is the leader of these enemy forces – not greatly different from Satan in Christian teaching (cp. 2 Cor. 6: 15).

The section ends by returning to narrative using the third person. The prophet announces the LORD's vengeance on his enemies. *consumed* fits the broader picture of destruction by fire. ✳

Israel and Judah rid of
the invaders

These are the words of the LORD:

Now I will break his yoke from your necks   13
    and snap the cords that bind you.
Image and idol will I hew down in the house of your   14
    God.
    This is what the LORD has ordained for you:
    never again shall your offspring be scattered;
    and I will grant you burial, fickle though you have
        been.
    Has the punishment been so great?   12
    Yes, but it has passed away and is gone.
I have afflicted you, but I will not afflict you again.

See on the mountains the feet of the herald   15[a]
    who brings good news.
Make your pilgrimages, O Judah,
    and pay your vows.
For wicked men shall never again overrun you;
    they are totally destroyed.
The LORD will restore the pride of Jacob and Israel alike,   **2** 2[b]
    although plundering hordes have stripped them bare
    and pillaged their vines.

[a] *2: 1 in Heb.*
[b] *Verses 1 and 2 transposed.*

✻ For the first time the prophet announces the LORD's own words. The passage addresses Judah (1: 12–13), and Belial (1: 14). The prophet then speaks to Judah again (1: 15) and Nineveh (2: 1). The final word does not use direct address as it predicts restoration for Israel (2: 2).

The key problem turns on deciding who is meant by 'you' and 'your' in the passage. The pronoun is feminine singular in 1: 12–13. In verse 13 this clearly refers to Judah. The fact that the translation of verse 12 is not easy makes the reference there uncertain. N.E.B. has treated it as related to Judah and moved the verse to follow verse 14. In verse 14 the pronoun is masculine singular, and is seen as a reference to Belial. In verse 15 it is again feminine singular and refers to Judah. In 2: 1 (moved in N.E.B. to open the next section) it is feminine singular but clearly refers to Nineveh.

13. *his yoke* means Judah's subjugation to Assyria. For more than a hundred years she had felt the pressure of Assyrian rule. She had had to pay tribute and submit to all sorts of indignities. She had known the invasion of Assyrian armies whenever she had taken a more independent line. God's word promises an end to all that.

14. Belial, or the Assyrian general, is addressed. The ultimate indignity which a state's divine patron can experience is decreed. The god's, or goddess's, temple will be stripped of its *image* and every *idol*. *offspring* is literally 'from your name'. The original may mean that he will have no more children. The details are obscure. What is clear is that this added one more picture of his coming annihilation. *fickle* translates a word that means 'light, of no consequence' and the phrase may be translated 'for you have become too weak'; in that case the reference to *burial* implies that he will have neither time nor strength to build his own tomb, as was the custom of great rulers.

12. *punishment:* as the verse is translated here, the punishment is the one meted out to Judah by the coming of the Assyrians as Isaiah prophesied. The verse would also have been

particularly meaningful to 'the Israel of the exile' which read these words after another punishment and another enemy had come upon Judah.

15. This verse begins a new chapter in the Hebrew text and it is thus understood as marking a new beginning (cp. Isa. 40). It joyfully exults in response to the prophetic announcement. In anticipation of the message that the prophecy has been fulfilled, he calls them to look to the road over the mountains for the *herald*. *good news* is literally 'tidings of peace'. He expects the announcement that the battle is over; the enemy has been overcome; peace has been restored. *pilgrimages* are for giving thanks and making new commitments of themselves to the LORD. *pay your vows* which were made in your prayers for deliverance. For *never again* shall Judah be *overrun* by Assyria as she had been so often in the past.

wicked men translates 'Belial'. The champion of Nineveh's might and Ishtar's power has been overcome by the word of the LORD. Israel need never again fear him or the powers he has served. *they:* singular in the Hebrew: 'he is totally destroyed'. This corresponds to the complete end that the LORD had promised for him in verse 9.

2: 2 *the pride of Jacob and Israel alike:* Samaria had also fallen to Assyrian power in 721 B.C. Her people had been deported and scattered over the Assyrian empire. Other exiles had been resettled on her land (cp. 2 Kings 17: 24). In Nahum's time it would have been quite fitting to expect that the result of Assyria's downfall would be a restoration of northern Israel as well as Judah. This was not to be. The northern exiles had apparently been absorbed in the lands to which they were sent. But prophetic faith never gave up the hope that God would complete his restoration of his people with all the tribes represented (cp. also Rev. 7: 4–8). ✳

Nineveh's enemies triumphant

✸ The rest of the book is devoted to the destruction of Nineveh. The first part (2: 1–12) describes the concluding battle. Then comes the LORD's curse that seals her doom (2: 13 – 3: 6). The concluding section (3: 7–19) is a taunting song about the doomed city. ✸

THE LAST BATTLE

1 The battering-ram is mounted against your bastions,
    the siege is closing in.
Watch the road and brace yourselves;
    put forth all your strength.
3 The shields of their warriors are gleaming red,
    their soldiers are all in scarlet;
    their chariots, when the line is formed,
    are like flickering[a] fire;
4 squadrons of horse[b] advance on the city in mad frenzy;[c]
they jostle one another in the outskirts, like waving torches;
    the leaders display their prowess[d]
5   as they dash to and fro like lightning,
    rushing[e] in headlong career;
they hasten to the wall, and mantelets are set in position.
6 The sluices of the rivers are opened, the palace topples down;

[a] flickering: *prob. rdg.; Heb. obscure.*
[b] squadrons of horse: *so Sept.; Heb.* the fir-trees.
[c] *Prob. rdg.; Heb. adds* chariots.
[d] display their prowess; *or* shout their own names.
[e] *Prob. rdg.; Heb.* stumbling.

the train of captives goes into exile,　　　7
　　their slave-girls are carried off,
moaning like doves and beating their breasts;
　　and Nineveh has become like a pool of water,　　8
like the waters round her, which are ebbing away.
'Stop! Stop!' they cry; but none turns back.

Spoil is taken, spoil of silver and gold;　　　9
　　there is no end to the store,
treasure beyond the costliest that man can desire.
　　Plundered, pillaged, stripped bare!　　　10
Courage melting and knees giving way,
writhing limbs, and faces drained of colour[a]!
　　Where now is the lions' den,　　　11
the cave[b] where the lion cubs lurked,
where the lion and[c] lioness and young cubs
　　went unafraid,
the lion which killed to satisfy its whelps　　　12
and for its mate broke the neck of the kill,
mauling its prey to fill its lair,
　　filling its den with the mauled prey?

✴ 1. This verse still belongs to the group of oracles which directly address someone. *your* is again a feminine pronoun that refers to Nineveh/Ishtar.

The previous section pictured the battle in the field. Now the war moves toward the fortresses of the city itself. The battle descriptions are those of a *siege* against the defences of a fortified city. *battering-ram* is literally 'he who (or, that which) scatters' and is often understood as a personal reference to the

[a] drained of colour: *mng. of Heb. uncertain.*
[b] *Prob. rdg.; Heb.* pasture.
[c] and: *prob. rdg.; Heb. om.*

LORD who had scattered the forces of Belial in the field and now mounts the battle against the city. The N.E.B. translation of the following lines sees them as exhortations to Nineveh. But the Hebrew may be understood with the LORD as subject:

> 'guarding the siege-works
> watching the way
> bracing himself
> gathering exceeding strength'

3. The personal address is dropped as the battle begins. The attacking forces move forward with *gleaming red...shields*, uniforms in *scarlet*, and *chariots...like flickering fire*. These may be very accurate descriptions of the armies gatherered before Nineveh for the assault. Leather shields were sometimes given a coat of a red substance to preserve their strength. It is possible that the armies of the Medes and the Babylonians did wear red uniforms. The polished metal of the chariots may have appeared as fire in the sun.

For the prophet the armies are also the forces of the LORD who appear as chariots of fire, coming with the force of the storm and with the devastation of the earthquake. They work within the processes of history. But they are also the armies of the great day of judgement which subdue the chaotic powers of evil (cp. Ps. 68: 17; Josh. 5: 13–15; Joel 2: 1–11).

In the previous section it was apparent that Nineveh and her patroness Ishtar were closely identified. Now the prophet sees the historical armies of the nations approaching Nineveh as the armies of the LORD. Above their visible and physical efforts and powers are the invisible supernatural forces of the LORD.

4. The battle begins and the armies move *on the city*. The outer defences have fallen and the struggle continues in the narrow lanes and alleys.

5. *display their prowess* is literally 'make their names to be remembered'. *rushing in headlong career* is literally 'they stumble in their going' which probably refers to over-eagerness in the attack. *the wall* is literally 'her wall'. As in the previous

chapter this may refer to Nineveh or to Ishtar. This inner wall of the city surrounds and protects the most important buildings, the seat of government, and the great temples. *mantelets* are the shelters set up to protect attackers from missiles thrown down from the walls. Preparations for the final assault are complete.

6. Then, instead of direct armed attack, another strategy is used: *The sluices of the rivers are opened.* The area is flooded, undermining the foundations of the city's buildings so that they collapse. This may be understood simply in military terms, but it may be that Nahum is here turning to the supernatural picture. The great cosmic waters are generally thought of as destructive powers. They had to be subdued and pushed back as part of the creation (Gen. 1: 6–9). They were God's instrument of destruction in the great flood (Gen. 7: 11; cp. also Job 22: 16; Isa. 8: 7). In this case *the rivers* are the currents of the great cosmic ocean (cp. 1: 4; Ps. 93: 3).

7. *train of captives* translates a difficult word: *huzzab*. This has sometimes been understood as a mysterious name for a god. Here it seems more likely to be something from the temple, perhaps the idol's pedestal. This implies the destruction of the idol itself in fulfilment of 1: 14. *their slave-girls:* the translation has again made a plural of a singular pronoun 'her'. This would fittingly refer to Ishtar whose temple had been destroyed, her image broken, and the base taken away as booty. The *slave-girls* or maidens are the sacred harlots who were an important part of the Ishtar cult. Normally they would dance in the temple; now they are marched away with gestures of grief.

8. *Nineveh:* the name of the city is mentioned here for the first time, except for the title. She is identified as the goal of the assault. The figure of water in verse 6 is now picked up. Nineveh's considerable strength and power had been like a great pool of water, always with ample reserves. But now that the streams have been loosed upon her (verse 6) they have overrun this pool. The walls or dykes of the pool have been

eroded. When *the waters round her* ebb after the flood, the waters of the pool disappear too. That is, the destruction of the city robs Assyria of the reserves of power and influence on which she had relied in the past. The picture may also imply that the troops desert and flee. *Stop!* efforts to try to halt the fleeing forces are in vain. They are totally demoralized.

9. *is taken:* the Hebrew verb is an active imperative: 'take plunder'. The booty from the city that was the capital of the world for so long is rich.

10. The disastrous end of the mighty empire is pictured in three resonant sounds that grow with each word. In Hebrew they have similar sounds: *Plundered, pillaged, stripped.* The next lines picture the collapse of human qualities which have made the city great in the past.

11f. This section is concluded with verses of derision in rhetorical questions (*Where now?*) using the metaphor of a pride of lions. Nineveh had been like a den to which her soldiers had brought the booty of the hunt. Those who remained behind had lived well on the *prey* of spoils and captives which were the results of countless military campaigns. But now the city showed no resemblance to the *lair* of the king of beasts. The figure of the lion is particularly good for the overtones of supernatural conflict in the book. Ishtar was often pictured mounted on a lion's back or even herself as a lioness. And the monstrous enemy of God in creation was often represented as a voracious lion.

The verses fittingly end this part of the picture of Nineveh's destruction. They stress the certainty that Assyria's hold of terror over the ancient East would be permanently broken. ✻

THE LORD'S CURSE ON NINEVEH

13   I am against you, says the LORD of Hosts,
  I will smoke out your pride,[a]
  and a sword shall devour your cubs.

[a] your pride: *prob. rdg.; Heb.* her chariot.

I will leave you no more prey on the earth,
and the sound of your feeding[a] shall no more be
heard.

Ah! blood-stained city, steeped in deceit,   **3**
full of pillage, never empty of prey!
   Hark to the crack of the whip,   2
the rattle of wheels and stamping of horses,
bounding chariots, chargers rearing,[b]   3
   swords gleaming, flash of spears!
The dead are past counting, their bodies lie in heaps,
corpses innumerable, men stumbling over corpses –
all for a wanton's monstrous wantonness,   4
   fair-seeming, a mistress of sorcery,
  who beguiled nations and tribes
   by her wantonness and her sorceries.
I am against you, says the LORD of Hosts,   5
  I will uncover your breasts to your disgrace
and expose your naked body to every nation,
  to every kingdom your shame.
I will cast loathsome filth over you,   6
I will count you obscene and treat you like excrement.

✻ This section has a total change of style. The LORD twice
announces his opposition (2: 13 and 3: 5–6). The city is
addressed in the second person feminine singular with which
the reader is already familiar. In between the prophet enunciates an oracle of woe.

13. The LORD's personal involvement is stressed in this
passage by the repeated use of I. He is further identified as
the *LORD of Hosts*. This is a military title which was familiar
to readers of the history of early Israel. It is regularly related

[a] your feeding: *prob. rdg.; Heb.* your messenger.
[b] chargers rearing: *lit.* men making their chargers rear.

to the Ark of the Covenant and to the occasions when Israel was called to holy war by such leaders as Joshua, Gideon, and Saul. *I am against you* challenges Nineveh with words which echo the tones with which a champion challenged his opponent on the field of battle.

The metaphor of the lion is resumed in *cubs* and *prey*. But it is not kept as consistently as the N.E.B. translation has made it. *pride* is literally 'chariot' and *feeding* is 'your messenger'. But even the mixture of metaphor with reality conveys the picture of doom that awaits the city against which God has announced his enmity.

3: 1 *Ah!* is often translated 'woe' and introduces a type of oracle in prophecy that was used more than a century earlier by Amos (e.g. Amos 5: 18f., in the Hebrew) and by Isaiah (e.g. Isa. 5: 8f.). It bewails the violence, deceit, and greed of the city.

2–3. The battle comes as a well-earned punishment.

4. *wanton* is simply 'harlot'. It refers to Nineveh, but it is suggested by the features of the cult of Ishtar, her patroness. As the goddess of sex and war, her temples were furnished with sacred prostitutes. She was even called a harlot in descriptions by some of her own worshippers. Stories of her exploits included acts of savagery and destruction. She was a most fitting symbol for the brutal empire. With lustful visions of riches and power Ishtar had *beguiled nations* into war and conquest. Like the Devil of Christian thought, she tempted and demonized all who came within her influence.

5. It is no wonder that the LORD announces: *I am against you*. He vows to disgrace her and reveal her *shame* (cp. Jer. 13: 22, 26f.; Ezek. 16: 36f.; Hos. 2: 3, 9).

6. An extreme curse is spoken which should prevent her ever being accepted among men again. ✳

A TAUNT SONG FOR THE DOOMED CITY

Then all who see you will shrink from you and say,   7
'Nineveh is laid waste; who will console her?'
Where shall I look for anyone to comfort you?
   Will you fare better than No-amon?–   8
      she that lay by the streams of the Nile,
      surrounded by water,
whose*a* rampart was the Nile, waters her wall;
Cush and Egypt were her strength, and it was bound-   9
      less,
Put and the Libyans brought her*b* help.
She too became an exile and went into captivity,   10
her infants too were dashed to the ground at every
      street-corner,
   her nobles were shared out by lot,
   all her great men were thrown into chains.
You too shall hire yourself out, flaunting your sex;   11
you too shall seek refuge from the enemy.
Your fortifications are like figs when they ripen: 12
if they are shaken, they fall into the mouth of the eater.
The troops*c* in your midst are a pack of women,   13
the gates of your country stand open to the enemy,
   and fire consumes their bars.
   Draw yourselves water for the siege,   14
      strengthen your fortifications;
down into the clay, trample the mortar,
      repair the brickwork.
   Even then the fire will consume you,   15

[a] whose: *so Scroll; Heb. om.*
[b] her: *so Pesh.; Heb.* you.
[c] *Or* people.

117

and the sword will cut you down.[a]
Make yourselves many as the locusts,
make yourselves many as the hoppers,

16 a swarm which spreads out and then flies away.
You have spies as numerous as the stars in the sky;

17 your secret agents are like locusts,
your commanders like the hoppers
which lie dormant in the walls on a cold day;
but when the sun rises, they scurry off,
and no one knows where they have gone.

18 Your shepherds slumber, O king of Assyria,
your flock-masters lie down to rest;
your troops[b] are scattered over the hills,
and no one rounds them up.

19 Your wounds cannot be assuaged, your injury is mortal;
all who have heard of your fate clap their hands in joy.
Are there any whom your ceaseless cruelty has not
borne down?

✳ The direct address as 'you' is continued. But apparently
the LORD's words have ended; the 'I' is not repeated. The
prophet continues, taunting the city with reminders of old
foes and of her present fatal weakness.

7. *console* means simply to express sympathy for her. All
the spectator nations note her fall. But no one is prepared to
comfort her, for they have all suffered from her power.

8. *No-amon* was Thebes, a powerful city of Egypt which was
conquered and plundered by Assyrian armies in 663 B.C. She,
like Nineveh, had been built by a river, the Nile, and her
defences were arranged accordingly. But they were not
enough to save her. The elaborate references to *streams* and

[a] *Prob. rdg.; Heb. adds* and consume you like the locust (*or* hopper).
[b] *Or* people.

water seem to go beyond a factual description of the city's position. The Egyptians thought of Thebes as a sacred city, built on the first dry land to emerge from the primeval waters. They considered the river Nile to be the supreme manifestation of creation's blessings, and based their faith and security on its powers. Nahum sees it, rather, as a symbol of their arrogant and heathen attitude against the LORD.

9. But No-amon had powerful allies and vassals. *Cush* lay to the south, possibly including what is today the Sudan as well as a good part of Ethiopia. *Put:* the term is used in the Old Testament to refer either to Somalia in the south or Libya in the west.

10. But these were not enough. She had experienced the practised arts of Assyrian brutality. The prophet does not interpret the fall of Thebes as a sign of Assyrian power. Rather, she was a symbol of what must happen to any nation that is against God.

11. Even the proud queen of the nations will do as the women of conquered cities had done: sell herself. The Hebrew for the second phrase means literally, 'you shall be a reserved one', that is, she will become a part of the army's brothel in exchange for a promise that she can live. Even Nineveh will have to *seek refuge from the enemy*.

12–13. The taunt derides Nineveh's strength which has turned to weakness: *fortifications* which are ready to fall, *troops* like women, *open...gates*, and *bars* that will burn easily.

14. The city is exhorted to exert itself as much as it can, and even that will be in vain, for she is doomed.

15. Assyria is compared to locusts that are destroyed in uncounted numbers, burnt with *fire* or crushed with swords.

16. *spies* is a word usually translated 'merchants'. The influence and power of a dominant country is shown in its commercial expansion as well as in the way its armies are deployed.

17. The comparison with locusts (verse 16) notes that they tend to reach a stage when they take wing and 'fly away'.

Assyrian forces are likened to these locusts. Their huge organization with *secret agents* and *commanders* has become useless. Under the heat of battle, the pressure of imminent defeat, they *scurry off* and cannot be found.

18. The *king of Assyria* is taunted with the picture of disintegrating morale in his officer corps. They are called *shepherds* and *flock-masters*, who were supposed to round up the troops and whip them into line. But now they *slumber* and take their ease. The troops have fled *over the hills* and no one can reassemble them.

19. The final verse sums up the *fate* of the king. It is as though the prophet stands over the fallen foe. He notes that his *injury is mortal*. He will die. This news will bring joy to all who hear it. No one will mourn. The prophet's rhetorical question wonders whether there is anyone who has not felt the burden of Assyria's *ceaseless cruelty*. ✳

✳   ✳   ✳   ✳   ✳   ✳   ✳   ✳   ✳   ✳   ✳   ✳   ✳

The prophecy ends with this taunt over the evil fallen foe of God. It is not relieved at the end with a reminder of Israel's restoration or of the glorious establishment of the reign of God like many other books. Both of these themes do occur earlier in the book.

The reader should keep the perspective of the book. Nineveh is no ordinary city for the prophet, nor is Assyria just another degenerating civilization. They stand for the ultimate supernatural evil that frustrates and suppresses the purposes and people of God. Their defeat is a sign of the victory of God and the basis for hope that his power and justice will ultimately conquer all evil.

✳   ✳   ✳   ✳   ✳   ✳   ✳   ✳   ✳   ✳   ✳   ✳   ✳

HABAKKUK

✡ ✡ ✡ ✡ ✡ ✡ ✡ ✡ ✡ ✡ ✡ ✡ ✡

THE TITLE

An oracle which the prophet Habakkuk received in a 1
vision.

✡ 1. *An oracle* (cp. comment on Nahum 1: 1). The use of the term here extends its meaning beyond its usual application to foreign nations. In Habakkuk it covers oppression both by a Judaean tyrant and by a foreign invader. This term is fitting for the first two chapters of the book. They are composed of two complaining prayers (1: 2–4; 1: 12–17) each of which is followed by an answer from God (1: 5–11; 2: 1–5). Then there are five passages of 'woe' (2: 6–8; 9–11; 12–14; 15–17; 18–20). A separate title introduces the third chapter.

the prophet: Habakkuk is given this title (Hebrew *nābī*) here and again in 3: 1, but it is rare in the headings of the prophetic books. Amos protested against having it applied to him (Amos 7: 14). The editors use it here with the phrase *received in a vision* to emphasize the immediacy and inspiration of this word from God.

Habakkuk: the name occurs only here and in 3: 1. It probably comes from the name of a plant, but there is no reason given for its being used for this man. Nothing is known of his life, his family, or place of origin. No date is given for the prophecy. The story of 'Daniel, Bel, and the Snake' in the Apocrypha has Habakkuk in an important role. He is carrying food to reapers in harvest time when an angel meets him. The angel seizes the hair of his head and takes him to Babylon where the food is given to Daniel in the lion's den (cp. Dan. 6: 10–24). Then the angel returns him to Judah. The beginning of that story, in a personal note, says that Habakkuk was a son of Joshua of the tribe of Levi. The many connections of the book of Habakkuk with worship support the view that he was one of the Levites who conducted temple worship in Jerusalem. Their usual duties included composing and arranging the prayers and psalms to be used in temple worship. Habakkuk's gift of prophecy was added to the skills normally required in his work. Through it the oracles of the book were *received* in that heightened sense of extraordinary consciousness which is here called being *in a vision*. *

DATE AND COMPOSITION

No hint is provided, in the heading, of the time Habakkuk lived and worked. Nor is there anything in the book by which it can be dated exactly. However, its position between Nahum and Zephaniah suggests a seventh-century origin.

The first oracle promises God's help by bringing the Chaldaeans (1: 6), i.e. the Babylonians who overcame Assyria in the last decades of the seventh century. In 609 B.C. Egypt marched through Judah on the way to fight against Babylon in the battle that finally ended Assyria's resistance. Josiah, Judah's great and good king, was killed in a skirmish with the Egyptians, and they appointed Jehoiakim as his successor. He ruled from 609 until 598 B.C. His reign was one of misrule and tyranny (2 Kings 24: 3–4) in which he gained power by currying Egypt's favour (cp. Jer. 22). In 605 Nebuchadnezzar defeated Egypt, but he did not consolidate his position immediately. For the next seven years Judah was caught in the power struggle of the two countries. In March 597 B.C. Nebuchadnezzar took Jerusalem a very short time after Jehoiakim was succeeded by his son, Jehoiachin. Ten years later the siege and fall of Jerusalem were repeated, the temple destroyed, and the monarchy came to an end.

The prayers of Habakkuk complain of violence, strife and tyranny. These words hardly describe the reign of Josiah who was such a popular and strong king from 640 to 609 B.C. They might fit the reign of Amon (642–640; cp. 2 Kings 21: 21) or that of Manasseh (697–642; cp. 2 Kings 21: 16), but both of these are too early for the mention of the Chaldaeans to be meaningful.

The reign of Jehoiakim was one in which strife and violence were commonplace (cp. 2 Kings 24: 2–4). At that time the announcement of the approach of Babylon would have been of great concern for the pro-Egyptian government of Judah.

But there has been no agreement among interpreters about this. The real villains have been thought by some to be Assyria or even Alexander the Great. Fortunately the greatness of the book does not depend on such historical identification. It may have deliberately avoided such, so that the poems could be repeated with meaning in other periods of distress. The original text contains many obscure or defective words. This is a problem for translator and interpreter alike as the large number of notes in ch. 3 of the N.E.B. indicates.

The continued influence of the book is shown by its being included in the canon. One of the first scrolls found in the ruins of the sectarian community of Qumran was a commentary on Hab. 1–2 which showed how the community interpreted it as though it prophesied their own history, a little before the time of Christ. The influence of the book on Paul is shown in his use of 2: 4 in such a decisive way (see p. 135).

This commentary will date the book in the reign of Jehoiakim in two parts: the first before 605 B.C. and the second shortly after that.

Divine justice

THE FIRST COMPLAINT

2 How long, O LORD, have I cried to thee, unanswered?
   I cry, 'Violence!', but thou dost not save.
3   Why dost thou let me see such misery,
          why countenance*a* wrongdoing?

      Devastation and violence confront me;
   strife breaks out, discord raises its head,
4   and so law grows effete;
         justice does not come forth victorious;
         for the wicked outwit the righteous,
         and so justice comes out perverted.

✵ 2. The prophet speaks as an individual, but he has composed this appeal to God on behalf of the entire community. This prayer of distress begins in the customary way: *How long, O LORD. cried* means 'cried for help'. *unanswered:* prayers for relief have been raised before, but the problem continues. The issue of unanswered prayer is particularly acute in the second prophecy (2: 2-4). The complaint uses the sacred name Yahweh (*LORD*) that was given to Israel to be used in prayer. It is presumably spoken now in the temple. The prayer thus fulfils the conditions of Solomon's plea that prayers spoken in this name and toward this place of God's dwelling would be answered (1 Kings 8: 28-53). Yet the burden of Habakkuk's complaint is that prayers have not been answered.

cry: this second use means 'call out' and the Hebrew adds 'to you'. *'Violence!'* is a call for help by a person being

[a] *Or* dost thou let me see *or,* with Pesh., do I see.

attacked. But God has shown no sign of hearing. He has certainly done nothing to *save* the petitioner. Yet the prophet turns again to the same God who has so far given no answer. This is typical of Old Testament faith (cp. Ps. 22 and Job). The belief that God is present even when he is not seen and that he is ultimately the basis of all hope is deeper than the impatience caused by his apparent unconcern for their present distress.

3. *Why?* the question is one that every age, and perhaps every person, asks at some stage. Jeremiah questions God like this at about the same time (Jer. 20: 18). Israel in exile cried out in confusion and anguish (Lam. 5: 20). Job asked it (Job 3). The question of why evil exists gets no answer, but the problem does have a solution. God provides it.

violence is defined more precisely by *Devastation*. *strife* is a legal complaint before a court. *discord* is a disagreement or quarrel. The verse pictures damage and harm done to the speaker which has led to a suit before the courts.

4. But in the courts *law* (literally *torah* or sacred law) proves feeble or slack (*effete*) and *justice does not come forth victorious*. It is not successful as a lasting solution. The courts fail to meet the problems posed by violence. In a legal contest *the wicked* are those who are at fault or guilty. *the righteous* are the innocent, those in the right.

The prophet complains that there is no order in society. This can only happen because of bad government or with the active connivance of the authorities. The LORD who made justice for all levels of society has a personal interest in justice. So an appeal to him is very appropriate. ✻

THE FIRST PROPHECY

Look, you treacherous people,[a] look:
 here is what will astonish you and stun you,
for there is work afoot in your days

5

[a] you treacherous people: *so* Sept.; Heb. among the nations.

which you will not believe when it is told you.

6   It is this: I am raising up the Chaldaeans,
that savage and impetuous nation,
   who cross the wide tracts of the earth
to take possession of homes not theirs.

7   Terror and awe go with them;
their justice and judgement are of their own making.

8   Their horses are swifter than hunting-leopards,
  keener than wolves of the plain;[a]
their cavalry wait ready, they spring forward,[b]
they come flying from afar
like vultures swooping to devour the prey.

9   Their whole army advances, violence in their hearts;
  a sea of faces rolls on;
they bring in captives countless as the sand.

10   Kings they hold in derision,
  rulers they despise;
they despise every fortress,
they raise siege-works and capture it.

11   Then they pass on like the wind and are gone;
and dismayed are all those whose strength was their god.

✵ 5. This verse calls attention to God's announcement in the next verse. *Look* translates two Hebrew words which mean 'see and take note'. The translation *you treacherous people* follows the Greek version (cp. footnote). The Hebrew has 'among the nations' which fits the context well enough; the difference lies in only one Hebrew letter. *treacherous people* translates a word which appears in two key passages in the book as 'traitors' or 'faithless ones'. In 1: 13 the complaint

[a] *Or* evening.
[b] they spring forward: *so Scroll; Heb.* their cavalry.

asks why God continues to countenance the 'treachery of the wicked'. In 2:5 the 'traitor', or faithless one, is contrasted with the faithful, righteous man.

If the historical setting is the last decade of the seventh century, the reference here is to the nobles of the court while that in 2:5 is to Jehoiakim himself. He and his friends in ruling positions were given power as Egyptian puppets. They never represented the real interests of Judah. By continuing to conspire with Egypt they courted Babylonian reprisal. They exploited the people and the land. The term 'faithless' or 'traitors' was most fitting.

It is no wonder that the announcement is expected to *astonish* and *stun* them. They had put their entire faith in Egypt. The rise of Babylonian power in west Asia would be a great blow to them.

6. *the Chaldaeans:* a century earlier Isaiah had announced that God was using Assyrian power to do his will (Isa. 7:17). Now a new prophet sees that he has chosen another Mesopotamian people. This prophecy belongs to the period between Nebuchadnezzar's defeat of Assyria in 609 B.C. and his campaign against Egypt in 605 B.C. Jeremiah supported this view that Babylon had been granted its authority by God in a prophecy spoken at the beginning of the reign of Zedekiah about 597 B.C. (Jer. 27:6). The extension and consolidation of their conquests followed the pattern which they inherited from Assyria.

7. *justice and judgement:* wherever they ruled, of course, the conquerors established their own law and justice.

8–10. The description becomes more stereotyped than historical. It is like pictures of the advance of God's armies in Isa. 5:26–30 and Jer. 4:13. Habakkuk sees the work of God behind the approach of Babylon's troops. The ultimate crisis which God will resolve is related to the events of history, but it is much deeper than anything which history alone can record. The advance is swift and takes in everything. There are *countless captives*. Nothing can stand in the conqueror's path. He sweeps away *Kings*, *rulers*, and fortresses.

11. This verse has been a problem for interpreters and translators alike. A literal translation of the first half reads: 'Then a spirit passed by and so he went on.' The N.E.B. takes the subject 'he' of the verb 'went on' to be the conqueror of the verses before. The text could mean that the spirit of God which sent them on this mission moved on. So the Babylonians passed by without disturbing the status of power in Jerusalem. This is apparently exactly what happened when they were on their way to attack Egypt in 604 B.C.

dismayed means that their hope and support is gone. *whose strength* can be understood as that of the one 'dismayed'. But it can also read: 'who made his strength their god'. In this case the strength is that of the Chaldaeans. They had failed to fulfil the hopes of those who had counted on them to overthrow the 'tyrants' in power. The text is too terse for us to be sure of the prophet's meaning.

The verse is a bridge to the next complaining prayer. From this prayer it is clear that the problems named in the first prayer are still unsolved. ✴

THE SECOND COMPLAINT

12   Art thou not from of old, O LORD?–
            my God, the holy, the immortal.[a]
        O LORD, it is thou who hast appointed them to execute
            judgement;
        O mighty God,[b] thou who hast destined them to chas-
            tise,
13   thou whose eyes are too pure to look upon evil,
            and who canst not countenance wrongdoing,
        why dost thou countenence the treachery of the
            wicked?

[a] the immortal: *prob. original rdg., altered in Heb. to* we shall not die.
[b] *Lit.* rock *or* creator.

Why keep silent when they devour men more right-
    eous than they?

Why dost thou make men like the fish of the sea,   14
like gliding creatures that obey no ruler?

They haul them up with hooks, one and all,   15
    they catch them in nets
    and drag them in their trawls;
then they make merry and rejoice,
sacrificing to their nets   16
    and burning offerings[a] to their trawls;
for by these they live sumptuously
    and enjoy rich fare.

Are they then to unsheathe the sword[b] every day,   17
to slaughter the nations without pity?

＊ This prayer of complaint begins with a recitation of what creeds and hymns say about God. Then it states the trouble-some question which disturbs the prophet and the people: How can the pure and holy God make use of such a violent and brutal force to do his work? Apparently the Chaldaeans have already shown their awesome power. But this has not changed the conditions the prophet lamented in his first prayer. Now he sees their headlong rush to power as the terrible thing that it is. He begins to doubt the correctness of the first prophecy which had announced that God himself had raised them up.

12. *Art thou not:* the words address God with a reminder of what faith holds that God is. The contrast in 'why?' (verses 13 and 14) shows a kinship to the questions of Jeremiah and Job. They all belong to an age that has begun to question God about his work with more frankness than earlier ages had dared. *O LORD:* the complaints and questions are directed to

[a] *Or* incense.
[b] unsheathe the sword: *so Scroll; Heb.* empty the net and...

God who had given his personal name and pledge to Israel. It is not to 'whatever gods there be' in the tones of doubt which that implies. These questions come from a troubled believer. The foundations of his faith are spoken in the words which he has sung in the hymns of the temple. *from of old:* God is everlasting. His work dates from earliest antiquity and before. Therefore he can be trusted now (cp. Deut. 33: 27; Ps. 74: 12).

my God: prayer's essential element is the claim to a relation with God which permits one to address him. *the holy:* Hebrew 'my holy one'. It seems strange that a mortal man should dare to call the holy one *my* God, but it is here that we may see the essence of religious certainty. *holy* implies separateness from mortal man and an independence of connections that would limit. Yet in the Old Testament this word often appears with a possessive pronoun which gives it a new meaning. Isaiah liked the term 'the Holy One of Israel'(e.g. Isa. 1: 4) which was used by psalmist and prophet alike (cp. Ps. 71: 22; Isa. 43: 15; Jer. 51: 5). So 'my holy one' lays claim to a personal relation to the eternal, holy, and immortal God.

thou who hast appointed them picks up the announcement of the first prophecy (1: 6). *them* is singular in Hebrew, but it is probably correctly understood as a collective for the Chaldaeans. *to execute judgement:* the prophet thinks of God's justice, although he had said the Chaldaeans had 'justice and judgement...of their own making' (1: 7). The problem lies exactly in this difference between God's justice and theirs.

O mighty God is literally 'O Rock', a term for God used frequently in the Psalms (e.g. Ps. 19: 14). It implies that he is reliable (as a rock is stable, cp. Ps. 31: 2) and protective (cp. Ps. 62: 7). God's direct responsibility for the work of the armies cannot be denied.

13. The address continues, citing God's purity and abhorrence of anything *evil* or of any *wrongdoing*. All these attributes of God the prophet acknowledges as true: antiquity, holiness, immortality, and purity. He recognizes God's concern for

justice, and his chastisement of those who do wrong. But then he states his problem.

why: it is not so much a question as a complaint. *countenance* means to see and condone. The prophet had just affirmed that God cannot *countenance wrongdoing*. Yet he shows no disapproval of this *treachery*. The word is plural in the Hebrew and could be translated 'traitors'. The reference may be deliberately vague to avoid direct reprisal by the king to whom it may refer or by the Babylonians whose acts are described in the following verses. The king would be 'faithless' if he betrayed the covenant with God by which he sits on David's throne. The Babylonians would be 'faithless' if they failed to do what God sent them to do.

keep silent means to let this happen without objection. The prophet is accustomed to having God act through his word or to reveal what is going to happen. But now God is silent. Jeremiah and Job struggled with the same problem.

devour: or swallow up. This word is common to complaints of this kind against oppressive acts. *wicked...righteous:* cp. comment on verse 4. But now the prophet complains that those who are in the wrong emerge victorious over those who are more entitled to be judged righteous. And God says nothing. It is as though lower courts have erred or been corrupted, but the high court makes no move to set aside the judgement or correct the error.

14. *Why* is not in the Hebrew, but the conjunction continues the sense of the previous verse. *men* means mankind. *obey no ruler* has the sense of 'have no leader'. The conditions pictured in 1: 3–4 of tyranny occurred in Judah because the people allowed the nation to be without a proper government. The prophet asks why God has made human nature to be so much like that of a *fish*.

15. The conquerors have taken advantage of this tendency to treat them as fish. Their military power deals with people the way fishermen use *nets* and *trawls*. It snares huge numbers of prisoners to put them to forced labour or to sell them in

the slave-market. Military conquest could be very profitable, giving reason for merriment among the successful 'fishermen'.

16. *nets* and *trawls* are the instruments of military might. The armies worshipped war and its instruments. In this sense their 'strength was their god', like those in I: II, and they worshipped accordingly. And well they might for these 'gods' supported a high standard of living for the soldiers and the state they represented.

17. But these things should be an affront to God. The prophet echoes the 'How long?' of I: 2. How long can the naked *sword* be allowed its sway? His indignation is not simply at crimes against Israel. How long will the *slaughter* of *the nations* be tolerated? *

THE SECOND PROPHECY

2   I will stand at my post,
I will take up my position on the watch-tower,
I will watch to learn what he will say through me,
    and what I shall reply when I am challenged.[a]

2   Then the LORD made answer:
Write down the vision, inscribe it on tablets,
    ready for a herald[b] to carry it with speed;[c]

3   for there is still a vision for the appointed time.
At the destined hour it will come in breathless haste,
    it will not fail.
    If it delays, wait for it;
    for when it comes will be no time to linger.

4   The reckless will be unsure of himself,
    while the righteous man will live by being faithful.[d]

[a] when I am challenged: *or* concerning my complaint.
[b] a herald: *lit.* one who can recite it.
[c] ready...speed: *or* so that a man may read it easily.
[d] *Or* by his faithfulness (*cp. Romans 1: 17; Galatians 3: 11*).

✻ 1. Having presented his challenge to God, the prophet pledges himself to be alert for a reply. As a watchman over Israel (cp. Isa. 21: 6, 8; Mic. 7: 7; Ps. 5: 3) his *post* is *on the watch-tower*. Isa. 50: 4–5 tells how God's servant is disciplined to be attentive to God's word in order to 'console the weary with a word in the morning'. Jeremiah waited ten days for the answer to a prayer he was asked to make (Jer. 42: 7). The prophet had no control of the inspiration which had him speak in God's name. His respect for God's freedom and sovereignty was complete. He could only be ready, to *watch* and *learn what he will say through* him. He was dependent on God and had to be prepared to obey. Only when God had spoken could he have a reply for those who asked.

2. Finally an answer begins. First come instructions and assurance that the answer will eventually arrive. *Write down the vision:* a basic question in the study of biblical prophecy is why the oracles came to be written. Isaiah was commanded to 'fasten up the message, seal the oracle among my disciples' (Isa. 8: 16; see N.E.B. footnote) because the fulfilment did not come immediately. Jeremiah had to dictate his messages so that they could be read in the temple because he had been banished from its precincts and could not deliver them personally (Jer. 36). But the usual forms of prophecy were delivered orally. The instruction 'to write down' his prophecy, though rare elsewhere, is given to Habakkuk. It may be motivated by the necessity of waiting for a full answer or by the continued relevance which the prophecy would have. The verses stress that there will be an answer. God will not be silent for ever. When he does speak a *herald* will be needed.

3. *there is still a vision:* God's silence might lead the people to feel that the age of prophecy is past. But the silence is neither proof that God is dead nor that he has no word. It is being reserved *for the appointed time*. God's choice of times is some-times difficult for men to understand or accept (cp. John 7: 6). With this the inspired answer to the complaint turns away from the question of why God acts as he does. It turns to the

question of how man behaves while he waits for God's answer or God's salvation.

This is the vital issue. In some sense men always live in the time between what God has already done and what faith expects him to do. The prophet had testified to the fulfilment of his earlier prophecy. God had raised up the Chaldaeans, as he had said he would. But what the prophet and the people had hoped would be the results had not come to pass. Their questions and complaints come from their disappointment. Faith in God is always trust that the answer *will come* at the right time. *it will not fail*, but it may delay. If it does, the response of faith is to *wait for it*. This waiting is the appropriate passive side of faith. There is another aspect of faith which calls for action. *when* the vision *comes*, active, obedient faith will be the order of the day.

4. Here is the inspired word for which he waited. It is one of the greatest verses in the Bible. Part of it is a word of judgement, and part an assurance of salvation.

The reckless: the Hebrew word is rare and may mean something like 'an audacious one'. But many interpreters judge it to be an error for a similar word which means one who has fainted or lost his senses (cp. Isa. 51: 20). *be unsure* is literally to be not straight, not level, or not right. This line refers to the one called 'wicked' or 'traitor' before. His conscious faculties will be stunned. The confidence which has characterized his arrogant oppressions will be gone. Lacking a trust in God, his self-centred life will disintegrate under pressure.

The second line speaks of those who have been oppressed and who have cried to God. *the righteous man* is without the article in Hebrew: 'a righteous one'. He is the one who is in the right with God and with his fellow men. *by being faithful:* his way of life in crisis continues in the ways that God has taught, even if he does not understand why God acts as he does or why there is no vision from God. *will live:* in contrast to the faithless one who, stunned and not right in his bearing, seems to approach the realm of death (cp. Ezek. 31: 15), the righteous man *will live*. He will be alive and vital, and he will keep a level head. This word maintains that God has not abandoned the believers in Israel. No matter how things look, the ones who go on believing and hoping in God will be the ones who eventually triumph, who will be saved to full life with God.

This line contains three words which are central to all biblical faith. *the righteous*, which originally meant only the winner of a legal contest, came to have a religious content as the person who is right in relation to God. He shares the 'being right' which only belongs to God and gladly grows in this 'rightness' by heeding God's instruction. He holds fast to God who is the only one totally 'in the right'. *faithful* translates a word with a basic meaning of being firm. It means to make oneself firm in God and in his way. It covers the meaning of trust and fidelity. *live* summarizes God's purposes in both creation and salvation. Others may only exist. But in God are the sources of abundant vitality. It covers the full range of natural and spiritual meanings.

This verse has had a tremendous influence. It is quoted by Paul in Rom. 1: 17 and Gal. 3: 11. It appears again in Heb. 10: 38. Its meaning in the New Testament has been coloured by its translation into Greek and by the particular concerns of the passages where it is used. Martin Luther made the verse in its New Testament sense the motto of the Reformation. Through its use the great doctrine of *sola fide* (by faith alone) became an even greater pillar of Christian faith.

Habakkuk is less concerned to define faith than is Paul and less concerned with a contrast to 'salvation by works' than Luther. He prescribes the attitude and way of life which the man 'in the right' with God will maintain in times of trial and crisis: he is neither to despair nor to straighten things out his own way. *by being faithful* he *will live* while some lie stunned and others destroy themselves.

Following this prophecy are five 'woes' spoken against the 'traitors' or 'tyrants'. They describe the contrasting conditions of the wicked in the judgement of God. Each of them is built up around a simple proverb-like sentence which may have been used to teach young people to avoid wrong behaviour. These are then interpreted almost like curses against oppressors.

The N.E.B. treats verses 5-8 as closely linked with verses 1-4. It seems better to treat them as a new unit; it begins with a strong particle meaning 'surely'. But we may recognize that it has probably been placed here to provide a comment on the preceding verses. ✳

THE FIRST WOE

5 As for the traitor in his over-confidence,[a]
  still less will he ride out the storm, for all his bragging.
  Though he opens his mouth as wide as Sheol
  and is insatiable as Death,
  gathering in all the nations,
  making all peoples his own harvest,

6 surely they will all turn upon him
  with insults and abuse, and say,
  'Woe betide you who heap up wealth that is not yours[b]
  and enrich yourself with goods taken in pledge!'

7 Will not your creditors suddenly start up,
   will not all awake who would shake you till you
    are empty,
  and will you not fall a victim to them?

8 Because you yourself have plundered mighty[c] nations,
  all the rest of the world will plunder you,
   because of bloodshed and violence done in the land,
  to the city and all its inhabitants.

[a] over-confidence: *so Sept.; Heb.* wine.
[b] *Prob. rdg.; Heb. adds* till when.
[c] *Or* many.

✻ The prophecy in 2:4 contrasted the way of 'the righteous' and 'The reckless'. In these passages the threats against the oppressors are made in the faith that evil will return upon those practising it, because God is just.

The first lines are confusing. Perhaps this was intentional. He speaks in riddles or proverbs. A literal translation would run something like this:

> 'Now if wine is a traitor,
>> a hero in self-confidence
>>> who never rests,
>>> who opens his mouth as wide as Sheol
>>> and is insatiable as Death,
>>> gathering in all the nations,
>>> making all peoples his own harvest,
>> will not all these raise a parable against him
>>> hinting at riddles for him, saying…'

5. Habakkuk appears to be quoting from traditional wisdom about the dangers of wine. The Qumran scroll's commentary on Habakkuk has a word similar to 'wine' which means 'wealth'. A warning about either is appropriate. But the closing lines concerning parables, allusive sayings, and riddles is a hint to look deeper into the meaning of the lines as the prophet develops them. *traitor* is the word already used in 1:5 and 1:13 to point to the source of the ills of which the prophet complains. The riddle of the wine is clearly about the tyrant king or the oppressing conquerors. The universal corrupting power of wine is easily applied to the Babylonians whose appetite is as great as *Sheol* (the place of the dead) or as *Death* itself. Their *harvest* includes all *nations* and *peoples*. If the N.E.B. rendering of 'over-confidence' instead of 'wine', which follows the Greek, is used, the passage applies directly to the traitor.

6. The plundered people *turn upon* him, whether these be the wine of the riddle or the villains of the application. They speak in parables, riddles, or obscure sayings, but the net effect

is *abuse*, *insults*, or even the stronger effect of curses which call down the judgement of God on them.

Woe betide you: this phrase begins each of the five sayings that follow. They each begin with a saying against a form of misconduct. Such series of statements were used in covenant ceremonies with the strong word 'A curse upon' (cp. Deut. 27: 14–26; 28: 16f.). But the use of the word 'woe' is only in the prophets. Amos (5: 18) and Isaiah (5: 8, 11, 18, 20, 22) used the word for a series of judgement speeches like these in Habakkuk.

The saying Habakkuk uses decries appropriating *wealth that is not one's own*. It denounces the violence or cunning by which someone makes himself rich with goods or money belonging to others. *goods taken in pledge* are things which have been deposited as security when people borrow money. Corrupt brokers put these to personal use (cp. Amos 2: 8). The law protected the borrower by restricting the deposit of coats as pledges (cp. Deut. 24: 6, 10–13).

7. The tables will be turned against the economic oppressor. The oppressed will *awake* to what is going on, and will *shake* him until he is separated from all his unjust gain. The evil corrects itself in having the wrongs come back to plague the doer.

8. Habakkuk now applies the saying to Babylon who had *plundered mighty nations*. The tables will be turned and her victims will *plunder* her.

The second half of the verse is a kind of refrain which appears again in verse 17. It sees this as judgement for desecration of the holy *land*, Canaan, the holy *city*, Jerusalem, and *all its inhabitants*, the people of God. ✻

THE SECOND WOE

9   Woe betide you who seek unjust gain for your house,
       to build your nest on a height,
       to save yourself from the grasp of wicked men!

Your schemes to overthrow mighty[a] nations   10
   will bring dishonour to your house
   and put your own life in jeopardy.
The very stones will cry out from the wall,
   and from the timbers a beam will answer them.   11

* 9. The first 'woe' was against those who wrongfully take personal gain. This one deals with the man who makes unjust profits to build a *house*. Through this fraudulent fortune he seeks security by building *on a height*. By these unjust means he tries to *save* himself from any calamity.

10. *to overthrow mighty nations* applies to either Jehoiakim or the Babylonians. These schemes will ruin all plans for security, bringing *dishonour*, or shame, on his *house*. Here house is used in the sense of his dynasty, making a word-play. And his own person will bear the guilt.

11. The prophet uses a very vivid picture. The building is so much the result of wickedness that even its materials cannot forgo protest. Jeremiah has a similar figure (Jer. 22: 13–14). *

THE THIRD WOE

Woe betide you who have built a town with bloodshed   12
   and founded a city on fraud,
   so that nations toil for a pittance,
   and peoples weary themselves for a mere nothing!   13
Is not all this the doing of the LORD of Hosts?
For the earth shall be full of the knowledge of the glory   14
   of the LORD
   as the waters fill the sea.

[a] *Or* many.

✻ 12. This passage draws on the resources of prophetic tradition. It moves one step higher to the one who wants to build a *town* or city (cp. Mic. 3: 10). Neither violence nor *fraud* can be the foundation for a lasting and healthy community.

13. *for a pittance* is literally 'only for the fire' (cp. Jer. 51: 58). The quotation originally referred to the futility of anxious activity which will all be in vain. It is here changed to refer to great efforts with slave labour to build a city which will amount to nothing. *the doing of the LORD:* the power is not simply the processes of retribution built into the social order. It is even more the direct control of events by God which prevents the permanent success of a way of life built on such violence and fraud.

14. *For* can also mean 'but'. In contrast to the fruitless work of forced labour is the inevitable fulfilment of God's purposes. The goal of history is not the building of cities by such means. The ancient story of those who built a tower to reach the heavens is also set in Babylon (Gen. 11: 1–9). God's goal concerns *the knowledge of the glory of the LORD* as he had announced to Moses (Num. 14: 21). It is a more universal goal than even his choice of a people or his gift to them of Canaan. *the glory* is the evidence of his holy presence. *knowledge* is the recognition and acceptance of that evidence (cp. Isa. 11: 9).

Habakkuk uses material from other prophets in slightly altered forms to show how God's purpose is itself a judgement on the oppressing nation and the tyrant king. ✻

THE FOURTH WOE

15 Woe betide you who make your[a] companions drink
   the outpouring of your wrath,

     making them drunk, that you may watch their
      naked orgies[b]!

[a] *Prob. rdg.; Heb.* his.
[b] naked orgies: *or, with Scroll,* appointed feasts.

Drink deep draughts of shame, not of glory;   16
you too shall drink until you stagger.[a]
The cup in the LORD's right hand is passed to you,
and your shame will exceed[b] your glory.

The violence done to Lebanon shall sweep over 17
you,
the havoc done to its beasts shall break your own
spirit,[c]
because of bloodshed and violence done in the land,
to the city and all its inhabitants.

✻ The figure of a drinking contest is turned into a picture of
the wrath of God in the form of a goblet of very strong drink.

15. The impersonal *Woe* denounces the debauchery which
uses a fellow's drunken stupor to strip him and abuse him
(cp. the story of Noah's drunkenness in Gen. 9: 20-5).

16. The saying notes that drunkenness tends more to
shame than to the *glory* which the drunkard imagines for
himself. Here the address is personal for the tyrant king or the
Babylonian enemy. The theme is developed around the idea
of the *cup* of the LORD's anger (cp. Obad. 16; Isa. 51: 17;
Ps. 75: 8). When the LORD's judgement comes, the great
nation will stagger like a drunkard and the shame of his deeds
will exceed his glory.

17. The atrocities of war return to burden the conqueror.
The magnificent forests of Lebanon were cut by the Assyrians
(Isa. 37: 24) and again by the Babylonians (Isa. 14: 8). The
trees made excellent timber for large buildings, but the forests
were destroyed in the process. The prophet is sensitive to the
loss of wild life (*beasts*) as well. The lines of verse 8 are repeated,
linking the guilt to *violence done* to God's *land* and to his *city*. ✻

[a] until you stagger: *so Scroll; Heb. obscure in context.*
[b] will exceed: *prob. rdg.; Heb. unintelligible.*
[c] shall break...spirit: *so Sept.; Heb. will indeed break.*

THE FIFTH WOE

18   What use is an idol when its maker has shaped it?–
      it is only an image, a source of lies;
  or when the maker trusts what he has made?–
      he is only making dumb idols.

19   Woe betide him who says to the wood, 'Wake up',
      to the dead stone, 'Bestir yourself'!*a*
  Why, it is firmly encased in gold and silver
      and has no breath in it.

20   But the LORD is in his holy temple;
      let all the earth be hushed in his presence.

✷ The topic is idolatry. The 'Woe' is preceded by a question deprecating idolatry. This derisive question anticipates by some eighty years the classic passage on the subject of idolatry in Isa. 44: 9–20.

18. *What use is an idol?* the self-deception inherent in idolatry is laid bare. It can only be a *source of lies*. Worse than nothing, idolatry is a false way.

19. It is therefore no wonder that a 'Woe' must be spoken on anyone who attempts to *Wake up* the *wood*, even if it is vain. The Hebrew has an additional phrase, 'He is a teacher', with the explanation: 'See. He is *encased in gold and silver.*' Both statements are apparently the idolater's support for his veneration. The last line of the verse may be better understood as a contrast: but it has no breath in it. *breath* translates a word which also means 'spirit'. An image has no life-force, nothing dynamic or alive about it. The distinguishing characteristic of the living God is that he is spirit and that he grants this life-spirit to those who worship him.

20. In contrast to the pitifully weak, shamed and discredited persons to whom the woes apply, God is real and present *in*

[a] *Prob. rdg.; Heb. adds* he will teach.

his holy temple. all the earth: from the earliest days of David's reign in Jerusalem God's rule on Zion was celebrated as a universal reign. The Psalms are full of praise to this kingdom. This verse echoes that language of worship (cp. Zeph. 1: 7; Zech. 2: 13). *in his presence* means being face to face with him.

The 'woes' on wicked people who have made themselves outlaws by their acts against moral laws and who rebelled against God and his people are brought to a close with this call to worship. The LORD has taken his place in Zion's temple. He is ready to judge the peoples and his people.

This verse prepares the way for the next chapter which is a prayer hymn addressed to the LORD who acts 'to save his people' (3: 13). ✲

A prayer for mercy

A prayer of the prophet Habakkuk.[a]　　　　　　　　**3**

✲ 1. A new title introduces the chapter. It is *A prayer* of supplication like, for example, Pss. 17 and 90. *of the prophet:* the combination of a term from the Psalms with *the prophet* shows how closely prophets were related to temple worship at this time (cp. commentary on 1: 1). Apparently the editors thought it necessary to identify the prayer with the prophet. It is a very appropriate climax for the prophecy which was related to temple worship in so many ways. The prophetic complaints and oracles fit the context of worship. They lead up to the great scenes of judgement. They take the themes of hymns and liturgy to make current applications to the needs of their day. Having done this, Habakkuk's prayer now moves back to the broader traditions of worship.

The Hebrew text has a note, '*al shigionoth*', which may indicate the tune or mood for the presentation of the prayer;

[a] So Pesh.; Heb. adds al shigionoth, *possibly a musical term.*

it probably suggests music suitable for a lament. Other musical notations appear through the prayer which cannot be translated. 'Selah' appears in verses 3, 9 and 13, as often in the Psalms. Its meaning is uncertain; it might be an instruction to the worshippers or to the musicians to play. Another at the end means something like: 'to the choirmaster: to be played on stringed instruments'.

Psalms like this were a regular part of worship. They were sung or spoken by choirs or individuals often with instrumental accompaniment. The presence of the prayer might be a sign that the entire prophecy was used in public worship.

The occasion most fitting for this was the great autumn festival which celebrated the renewal of God's covenant with his people and his world. Prayers were offered for the return of the rains and for deliverance from political and social problems. God was pictured as the victor over all enemies of order and of life in nature and in history. Through his victory full life was granted to the worshipper, his environment and his people. In this way Israel expressed its belief in God as the only source of life in nature or in the social order.

The prayer begins with a confession of faith (3: 2). It then pictures God's triumphant arrival and the abject submission of nature's greatest forces (3: 3–11). He is then seen in victory over the nations (3: 12–14). It closes with a three-fold personal response from the worshipper (3: 15–19). ✵

CONFESSION OF FAITH

2   O LORD, I have heard tell of thy deeds;
      I have seen,[a] O LORD, thy work.[b]

        In the midst of the years thou didst make thyself
          known,
      and in thy wrath thou didst remember mercy.

[a] *Prob. rdg., cp. Sept.; Heb.* I feared.
[b] *Prob. rdg.; Heb. adds* in the midst of the years quicken it.

✻ 2. The prophet speaks on behalf of the congregation – *I have heard*. But the phrases are intensely personal and individual. The mighty deeds of God had already been recited. Some of these were the same as those rehearsed in the next section. Others may have told the stories we know in the first seven books of the Bible. *I have seen* indicated a visual presentation of these events through drama, mime, or ritual. The worshipper confesses that these are truly the work of God and that he is what he has been represented to be. This translation as *seen* is a slight change from the Hebrew and is justified by its close parallelism with *heard*. The literal translation is, 'I fear, O LORD, thy work.' This is also a fitting phrase. Worship in the presence of the living God is an experience of fear and trembling for any mortal man.

In the midst of the years: the stories and pictures of God often make him seem so long ago or so far away that he has little to do with the here and now. This prayer is for God to reveal himself and his deeds now. The autumn festival was celebrated as a New Year's feast. God met the people there between the year that was past and the one that was to come.

The N.E.B. has omitted an important sentence (cp. footnote). 'in the midst of the years' occurs twice. The first time it is followed by 'quicken it' which may also mean 'make him live'. The following verbs can also be read as imperatives, making a prayer in three parts:

> 'In the midst of the years give him life.
> In the midst of the years make known.
> In wrath remember mercy.'

'Give him life': the life-giving meaning of the time 'between the years' is stressed. This could refer to the people or to all nature. But its most natural reference is to the king, David's son, the anointed one (or 'Messiah', cp. verse 13), who represented the entire people in the liturgy. In his life the people were also revived. *make...known:* God's purpose in coming includes revelation as well as life-giving deliverance.

The Hebrew verb has no object, neither 'it' nor 'you'. If one understands the object as *thyself*, as a self-revelation of God, the meaning is clear. But if the 'him' of the previous verb is the object, this is a prayer for God to make clear that the king is his agent on earth, his 'son' (cp. Ps. 2), through whom his will for the nations will be accomplished. A third possibility is to understand 'it' as object. This would mean 'make known the renewal of life'.

in...wrath: thy is not in the Hebrew. The festival drama demonstrated God's overwhelming power against all his enemies in the universe, among the nations, and even in Israel. This was the *wrath*. The dramatic ritual also had a place for *mercy*. This expression of God's warm affection and care was revealed to Abraham and promised to his descendants. The relation of wrath and mercy is most clearly seen in Exod. 34: 6. Habakkuk's prayer appeals to God to *remember* this facet of his relation to man. ✳

GOD'S APPROACH

3   God comes from Teman,
    the Holy One from Mount Paran;
  his radiance overspreads the skies,
  and his splendour fills the earth.

4   He rises[a] like the dawn,
      with twin rays starting forth at his side;
   the skies are[b] the hiding-place of his majesty,
   and the everlasting[c] ways are for[d] his swift flight.[e]

5   Pestilence stalks before him,
  and plague comes forth behind.

[a] He rises: *so Sept.; Heb. obscure.*
[b] the skies are: *prob. rdg.; Heb. there is.*
[c] *Or* ancient.
[d] and...are for: *transposed from end of verse 6.*
[e] his swift flight: *transposed, with slight change, from verse 7.*

He stands still and shakes the earth,   6
he looks and makes the nations tremble;
   the eternal mountains are riven,
   the everlasting*a* hills subside,
   the tents of Cushan are snatched away,*b*   7
   the tent-curtains of Midian flutter.

✲ 3. *God:* the old poetic term *Eloah* appears here. *Teman* may be the name of a place in the wilderness south of Canaan or it may mean simply 'the south'. *Mount Paran* is also located in territory to the south of Judah. These are in the area through which Israel travelled when they came from Sinai. God is pictured as he *comes* from that direction. The Old Testament faith in God's continuous presence on Zion did not prevent their holding a dynamic view of his movement. They sensed that he was 'present' at some times and in some events in a way in which he was not 'present' at others. *the Holy One* was used in 1: 12 in a call for God's intervention. Here it emphasizes the full participation of God in the events to follow. God's coming is accompanied by *radiance* and *splendour*. *the skies*, or heavens, and *the earth* together describe all the space there is.

4. God's approach is like that of the sun (cp. Ps. 19: 5–6). *twin rays* may picture lightning (cp. verses 9 and 11). *hiding-place* is literally a covering or veil for his power or *majesty*. *the everlasting ways* or 'the paths of eternity' are said to belong to him. They have sometimes been understood to be the paths of the stars through space.

5. *Pestilence* and *plague* appear almost like demonic figures that move *before him* and *behind* (literally 'at his feet'). It is unlikely that these are his attendants. Wherever he goes these move away like small animals or insects which scatter at a man's approach.

[a] *Or* ancient.
[b] are snatched away: *prob. rdg.; Heb.* under wickedness.

6. The reaction of the greatest and most solid things in nature shows God's omnipotence. Just standing still *shakes the earth*. A look is enough to make *the nations tremble*. *mountains* and *hills* are symbols of what is apparently *eternal* and *everlasting*, but they are split and levelled by God's approach.

7. Like a wind that blows down Bedouin *tents*, God moves through the wilderness. *Cushan* is probably the Sudan. *Midian* is land east of the Gulf of Aqaba. ✶

THE BATTLE

8   Art thou angry with the streams?[a]
         Is thy wrath against the sea, O LORD?
         When thou dost mount thy horses,
          thy riding is to victory.

9   Thou dost draw thy bow from its case[b]
         and charge thy quiver with shafts.[c]
         Thou cleavest the earth with rivers;

10–11   the mountains see thee and writhe with fear.
         The torrent of water rushes by,
         and the deep sea thunders aloud.
         The sun forgets to turn in his course,[d]
         and the moon stands still at her zenith,
         at the gleam of thy speeding arrows
          and the glance of thy flashing spear.

12   With threats thou dost bestride the earth
         and trample down the nations in anger.

13   Thou goest forth to save thy people,

[a] *So some MSS.; others add* or with the streams.
[b] Thou...case: *prob. rdg.; Heb.* Thy bow was quite bared.
[c] and...shafts: *prob. rdg., cp. Luc. Sept.; Heb.* weeks, shafts, word.
[d] The sun...course: *prob. rdg.; Heb.* The sun raised the height of his hands.

  thou comest[a] to save thy anointed;
thou dost shatter the wicked man's house from the
     roof down,[b]
uncovering[c] its foundations to the bare rock.[d]
Thou piercest their[e] chiefs with thy[f] shafts, 14
and their leaders are torn from them by the whirl-
     wind,
  as they open[g] their jaws
to devour their wretched victims in secret.

✳ 8. The prayer asks against whom God's anger is directed.
At the beginning of time he had fought against *the sea* as
the vision of ancient cosmic battle portrayed it. The waters
often symbolize all opposition to God. *When* can also be
translated 'for'. Whenever God enters the battle, his goal is
victory over these forces. *victory* is literally 'salvation'. It is
the victory that brings order in place of chaos, life instead of
death.

9. The battle is joined. The storm breaks as lightning flashes.
The heavy rain cuts the land with *rivers*.

10. *mountains, water* and *sea* are convulsed with *fear*. Even
the *sun* and *moon* stand still.

12. The picture turns from nature to history. God's anger
is now seen to be against *the nations*.

13. Here is the answer to the question in verse 8. God
intervenes *to save* his *people*. The vision is an answer to the
prophet's complaints. God's entire power is committed to

[a] thou comest: *prob. rdg., cp. Arabic version; Heb. partly lost.*
[b] the wicked...down: *prob. rdg.; Heb.* a head from the house of the
wicked.
[c] *So Vulg.; Heb.* bare places.
[d] bare rock: *prob. rdg.; Heb.* neck.
[e] their: *prob. rdg.; Heb. om.*
[f] *Prob. rdg.; Heb.* his.
[g] from them...open: *prob. rdg.; Heb. obscure.*

the battle against the oppressor. *to save* is the same word that was translated 'victory' in verse 8. God's goal is salvation for his people.

thy anointed: this reference to the Davidic king who reigned in Jerusalem is a reminder that he was a key participant in these festivals. Salvation for the people was closely bound up with that of the king. He was the LORD's 'anointed' (Hebrew *māshiaḥ* = messiah). God had promised David that one of his descendants would always be on the throne even if God had to chastise him for his faults (cp. 2 Sam. 7: 12-16). Such chastisement and subsequent 'salvation' were probably portrayed in the ritual as numerous royal Psalms suggest (e.g. Ps. 89).

For Habakkuk this relation of king and people must have been a problem. Jehoiakim was apparently the cause of much of the prophet's distress. However that may be, the faith of the prophet and of the people in Zion held firmly to God's promise to save his anointed and through him or his successor to save and bless the people. *the wicked man* is anyone who opposes God, his anointed, or his people.

14. God's vengeance breaks upon the oppressors while they are still engaged in their terrible acts devouring *wretched victims*, as they think, *in secret*. ✶

RESPONSE

15   When thou dost tread the sea with thy horses
        the mighty waters boil.
16   I hear, and my belly quakes;
        my lips quiver at the sound;
        trembling comes over my bones,
        and my feet[a] totter in their tracks;
            I sigh for the day of distress

[a] my feet: *prob. rdg., cp. Sept.; Heb.* which.

to dawn over my[a] assailants.

  Although the fig-tree does not burgeon,   17
  the vines bear no fruit,
  the olive-crop fails,
the orchards yield no food,
the fold is bereft of its flock
  and there are no cattle in the stalls,
yet I will exult in the LORD   18
  and rejoice in the God of my deliverance.
The LORD God is my strength,   19
who makes my feet nimble as a hind's
  and sets me to range the[b] heights.

* 15. The prayer turns back to express a personal response of the worshipper. When God moves in warlike ways, even *mighty waters boil* in response. How much more then is the response of the faithful.

16. He experiences the total emotions of fear and dread. But his emotions do not prevent his prayer, a *sigh for the day of distress* (i.e. the day of the LORD) *to dawn over* his *assailants*. These are literally 'the people who attack us'. This prayer-sigh returns to the pleas of 1: 12–17.

17. The prophet is confident of God's victory. He lives by the 'word' which God has given that 'the righteous man will live by being faithful' (2: 4). He believes in the saving work of God which will return fertility to the fields and life to the people, although there is as yet no sign of that change.

18. *yet I* places the singer in the ranks of faithful believers. Joy is the fruit of faith and hope. Its roots are in God rather than in what God has given. He is *the God of my deliverance*. He was shown to march triumphantly to salvation in his battle with the great cosmic forces (3: 8). He campaigned for

[a] *So Targ.; Heb.* his.
[b] *So Sept.; Heb.* my.

the salvation of his people and his anointed (3: 13). The singer confesses that God's victory also brought about his personal salvation.

19. The confession reaches its climax in using the strongest names for God at his disposal: *The LORD God.* The Hebrew is 'Yahweh, my Lord' which links the traditions of covenant assurance with personal dedication and commitment. *my strength:* the word means capacity, property, or armed might. The prophet confesses Yahweh, his Lord, to be his all: potential, wealth, and security.

The closing lines are like those in Ps. 18: 33. Life based on the LORD's salvation is one of joy and freedom like that of a graceful deer (*a hind*) that leaps easily on *heights* that would be fearful for any other creature. ✶

✶ ✶ ✶ ✶ ✶ ✶ ✶ ✶ ✶ ✶ ✶ ✶ ✶

ZEPHANIAH

✳ ✳ ✳ ✳ ✳ ✳ ✳ ✳ ✳ ✳ ✳ ✳ ✳

THE TITLE

THIS IS THE WORD OF THE LORD which came to **1**
Zephaniah son of Cushi, son of Gedaliah, son of
Amariah, son of Hezekiah, in the time of Josiah son of
Amon king of Judah.

✳ This form is used in Hosea, Joel and Micah. It introduces the
book as a message from God which has been entrusted to a
particular person.

Zephaniah: nothing is known about this man beyond what
is in this verse. Other people by this name do appear in the
Bible. In its present form the name means 'the LORD protects'.
But the original meaning was probably a confession 'Zephan
is Yahweh'. Zephan was an important Canaanite god who
gave his name to 'Zaphon', the mythical mountain home of
the gods. Hebrew used this word to mean 'the north'. The
name confesses that Zephan is identical with the LORD, but
this old meaning may have been long forgotten when the
traditional explanation took its place.

The number of names tracing the prophet's descent is
unusual. If Hezekiah at the end of it was the great king of
Judah who reigned from 715 to 687 B.C., this could explain
it. Zephaniah's heritage would then explain his concern for
genuine royal traditions in Jerusalem. His father's name,
Cushi, means 'Ethiopian' which suggests a partial African
heritage. Moses' marriage to a Cushite woman caused quite
a stir (Num. 12: 1). During Zephaniah's lifetime it was
an Ethiopian Ebed-melech on the palace staff who saved

Jeremiah's life and received a promise from God (Jer. 38: 7–13; 39: 15–18).

in the time of Josiah (640–609 B.C.): this great king was responsible for major reforms (cp. 2 Kings 22–3; 2 Chron. 34–5). Zephaniah's condemnation of the very practices which Josiah changed may indicate that he prophesied early in that reign. His words may have influenced the king's decisions for reform.

son of Amon (cp. 2 Kings 21: 19): this note is a reminder of past history which determined so many of the conditions of Zephaniah's time (cp. the introduction, p. 9). Amon's reign was brief. He was murdered in a palace revolution. But the revolutionaries were put down by a new political force in Judah called 'the people of the land'. These citizens of Judah rose against the Assyrian sycophants of the royal staff to restore a king of David's lineage to the throne. They continued to be a significant political factor throughout Josiah's reign, providing his main support in the reforms of 626 B.C. They co-operated with Josiah in the reformation which intended to make Judah the people of God that Moses and David had envisaged. The book of Deuteronomy came to be the statement of their goals.

Success for Zephaniah's call for a changed worship, as well as the programme put forward by 'the people of the land', had to wait until the tide of Assyrian power began to ebb. This commenced during the reign of Asshurbanipal (669–626 B.C.). Josiah and the levitical and prophetic leaders of Judah had their programme for independence ready, too.

Zephaniah agreed with many of their views. He joined them in the fight against foreign influences, especially in religious matters. He saw the principal sins to be the worship of false gods. But Zephaniah at heart remained one with the great eighth-century prophets, and he was especially close to Isaiah. He believed pride to be the major sin of man, leading to rebellion against the authority of God. He proclaimed that God's judgement would be universal. Hope lay only beyond that great judgement day. In this he differed from those who believed that reformation which brought obedience to the Mosaic covenant could ensure peace and prosperity for Judah.

Zephaniah was thus a bridge between the eighth-century prophets of judgement and the prophets after the exile who preached the coming salvation of God. He marked the way for strong prophecies of judgement to gain a place in the worship of Zion's temple. He set the pattern for his successors, Nahum and Habakkuk, as well as later for Joel and Obadiah.

Interpreters have sometimes thought that parts of the book of Zephaniah were added to it at a much later date. It seemed impossible that one man spoke words of judgement and words of assurance in the way the book records them. Current studies of worship and prophetic forms in Judah during the seventh century find less difficulty in combining the two. It is possible that Zephaniah planned the entire prophecy for presentation in temple services within the decade before Josiah's reform in 626 B.C. ✳

Doom on Judah and her neighbours

A UNIVERSAL HARVEST OF EVIL

I will sweep the earth clean of all that is on it,   2
> says the LORD.
I will sweep away both man and beast,   3
I will sweep the birds from the air and the fish from
> the sea,
> and I will bring the wicked to their knees[a]
and wipe out mankind from the earth.
> This is the very word of the LORD.

[a] I will bring…knees: *prob. rdg.*; *Heb.* the ruins with the wicked.

4   I will stretch my hand over Judah
      and all who live in Jerusalem;
   I will wipe out from this place the last remnant of
         Baal
        and the very name of the heathen priests,[a]
5   those who bow down upon the house-tops
        to worship the host of heaven[b]
        and who swear by Milcom,
6   those who have turned their backs on the LORD,
      who have not sought the LORD or consulted him.

✳ 2-3. The LORD speaks his own threat against all the habitable world. *I will sweep...clean* may better be rendered, 'I will again sweep clean'. In terms which fit the scene of harvest he threatens destruction for *the earth*, all cultivable land.

The prophecy speaks in terms like those of Noah's flood even in the choice of words (cp. Gen. 6-8). The Bible thinks of all creation being related to the destiny of man. It shares the results of man's sin and will share in his ultimate redemption. Zephaniah's new word from God seems intended to replace the promise of Gen. 8: 21. *mankind* has a very negative sense parallel to *wicked*. The book has an ominous beginning. The word rendered *sweep clean* is also the word for 'ingathering' in the name of the autumnal festival, known as Ingathering (Exod. 23: 16) or Booths. Zephaniah's words provide a negative interpretation of the theme. In that festival Jerusalem was celebrated as the place of the LORD's throne from which he judged all the world. In the prophecy of Zephaniah the LORD begins with four threats against Jerusalem (1: 4-13). A description of 'the day of the LORD' (1: 14 - 2: 4) precedes oracles against the nations (2: 5 - 3: 10). Prophecies of hope and salvation conclude the book (3: 11-20).

[a] *So Sept.; Heb. adds* together with the (legitimate) priests.
[b] *So Sept.; Heb. adds* those who worship, who swear by the LORD.

4. *stretch my hand* means to point toward someone preparatory to punishing him. *over* is properly 'against'. *Judah:* here judgement is on the whole people, though Zephaniah's attention is primarily on *Jerusalem*. He is particularly concerned with judgement on *all who live* there. It was the place where a foreign way of life had taken root. Government officials had the most contacts with Assyrians and the most pressure to adopt their ways. *from this place* refers to Jerusalem where the LORD had the temple as his home. *the last remnant* is specifically the survivors of the worshippers of Baal. This is the title, meaning 'lord' or 'husband', given to the most popular of the Canaanite deities who served as a weather and fertility god. Israel tended to identify the LORD with him during their early period in Canaan. But Elijah made Israel face the choice of the LORD or Baal, with no compromise allowed. Hosea forbade Israel ever to use 'Baal' as a title for the LORD again (Hos. 2: 16).

heathen priests were priests serving idols. The Hebrew adds 'together with' (or we might read 'from among') 'the (legitimate) priests' (cp. footnote). The verse calls for cleansing the priesthood of all who had served idols. Josiah is reported to have done exactly this (cp. 2 Kings 23; 2 Chron. 34).

5. The apostate priests worshipped on their house-tops, which were open to *the host of heaven*, the stars, which were their gods. 'those who worship, who swear by the LORD' has been left out of the translation (cp. footnote). But it could make good sense in either of two ways. Following this rendering with 'swear' for the verb, we get a condemnation of those who worship the LORD and Milcom at the same time. But the same Hebrew letters as are rendered 'swear' (*shaba'*) could be read to mean 'be fed by' (*saba'*). The passage may intend a word-play on these similar words: 'those who bow down, who are fed by the LORD, but who swear by Milcom'. This would picture priests whose support comes from their service in the temple of the LORD but whose genuine commitment is to a foreign deity.

swear by: oaths were a form of worship. In every oath a person made a public confession of his faith in the god he named. *Milcom* is properly 'their *melek*', that is, 'their king'. This is the name or title of a major Canaanite god known as Athtar in Ugarit, as Chemosh in Moab, or as Milcom in Ammon. Athtar was associated with the planet Venus. He was therefore one of the astral deities mentioned in verse 5.

6. These priests are accused of breaking the first commandment which prohibits having other gods 'to set against' the LORD (cp. Exod. 20: 3). When they did this, they *turned their backs* and ignored the LORD in his own city. ✶

THE DAY OF THE LORD – I

✶ The first section on 'the day of the LORD' contains an introduction (verse 7) and three parts each beginning with similar words (verses 8–9, 10–11, 12–13) which describe things that will be part of that great event. ✶

7   Silence before the Lord GOD!
      for the day of the LORD is near.
    The LORD has prepared a sacrifice
      and has hallowed his guests.

8   On the day of the LORD's sacrifice
    I will punish the royal house and its chief officers
    and all who ape outlandish fashions.

9   On that day
    I will punish all who dance on the temple terrace,
  who fill their master's[a] house with crimes of violence
      and fraud.

✶ 7. *Silence:* the Hebrew word sounds like 'hush' (cp. Hab. 2: 20). *before* indicates that an announcement has just been made that God is present in his temple. *the Lord GOD:* cp.

[a] *Or* their Lord's.

the commentary on Hab. 3: 19. *for the day of the LORD is near:* cp. the commentary on this announcement in Joel 1: 15 and 'The form and role of foreign prophecy' on pp. 5–6. *a sacrifice:* the word refers to 'slaughter' which may be for sacrifice, but which can equally well be used for the preparation of a meal in which meat will be served. Since the LORD himself has *prepared* it, the idea of a feast is better. To be *hallowed* is to prepare for service to God. It requires being set apart or cleansed. *guests* are those who have been called. Such guests may be 'set apart' (cp. 1 Sam. 16: 5). The words are also those used in 'holy war' in which God himself participates in the battle. The 'day of the LORD' draws on descriptions of such warfare and this may be the reference here (cp. comment in Obadiah pp. 6of.).

8. *day…sacrifice:* the two terms for the great occasion are brought together. This is undoubtedly the great festival day on Zion. The guests are worshippers in the temple. *sacrifice* or slaughter has a double meaning like that in Jehu's invitation to the worshippers of Baal (2 Kings 10: 19–24). *the royal house* is literally 'the sons of *melek* (king)', but this could be a reference to the god Melek, so that the *chief officers* would be the cult officials of Melek; this would continue the theme of alien religious practice. To *ape outlandish fashions* is to put on foreign clothes which were heathen garments used in worship (cp. 2 Kings 10: 22).

9. *temple terrace:* the elevated platform on which the inner temple building was built, with steps leading to it on all sides. *dance* may better mean 'climb up on'. The sin is in climbing up to the Holy of Holies or up on the altar platform (cp. Exod. 20: 24–6). This was probably a common practice in the worship of the stars. *their master's house:* another translation has been suggested: 'who fill the house (the temple) with "their lords", false and fraudulent', i.e. another reference to alien deities. (The N.E.B. footnote takes it as a singular, 'their Lord's', which is also possible.) This translation keeps the entire passage on one subject. Passages like 2 Kings 21;

Jer. 7: 30; 12: 11 and Ezek. 8 show that this picture of the temple in that time may be very realistic. ✲

10   On that day, says the LORD,
          an outcry shall be heard from the Fish Gate,
              wailing from the second quarter of the city,
          a loud crash from the hills;
11   and*[a]* those who live in the Lower Town*[b]* shall wail.
          For it is all over with the merchants,
              and all the dealers in silver are wiped out.

✲ This passage is a prophetic form based on the familiar call to lament (cp. Joel 1: 5–12).

10. *shall be heard* should probably be, 'let an outcry be heard'. *Fish Gate:* this and the other places cannot be located exactly. Some interpreters think they all lay on the north side of the city from which an attack would come.

11. *shall wail* is clearly an imperative in Hebrew: 'let those...wail!' *merchants:* the judgements on false worshippers will strike merchants and bankers who have profited by catering for worshippers in the sale of figurines and cult objects. *dealers in silver* may simply be 'all bags of money'. ✲

12   At that time
          I will search Jerusalem with a lantern
          and punish all who sit in stupor over the dregs of their
                  wine,
              who say to themselves,
          'The LORD will do nothing, good or bad.'
13   Their wealth shall be plundered,
              their houses laid waste;

[a] and: *prob. rdg.; Heb. om.*
[b] Lower Town: *lit.* Quarry.

they shall build houses but not live in them,
    they shall plant vineyards but not drink the wine from
        them.

✻ The direct address in God's own words continues, but the style changes to include an indictment in verse 12 and an announcement of judgement in verse 13. The charges are drunkenness and unbelief.

12. *with a lantern* may have been inspired by the torch-light processions which threaded their way through the dark streets on the nights of festival or by the myth in which the goddess Anath searches the underworld for her dead brother. But it is more likely that Prov. 20: 27 provides a better parallel: 'The Lord shines into a man's very soul, searching out his inmost being.' The lantern's light reveals men in *stupor* who sit in dark corners and drink their lives away. They think life has no meaning anyway since God *will do nothing, good or bad.*

13. Such people will discover that God does 'punish' them. The punishment takes two forms. In one, the wealth and property which has been their security will be violently removed. The second will be the operation of a principle which in the normal order of things deprives a drunkard of the reward of his efforts (cp. Amos 5: 11). ✻

THE DAY OF THE LORD – II

The great day of the Lord is near,
    it comes with speed;
no runner so fast as that day,
    no raiding band so swift.[a]
    That day is a day of wrath,
    a day of anguish and affliction,

14

15

[a] no runner…swift: *prob. rdg.; Heb.* hark, the day of the Lord is bitter, there the warrior cries aloud.

a day of destruction and devastation,
a day of murk and gloom,
a day of cloud and dense fog,

16   a day of trumpet and battle-cry
over fortified cities and lofty battlements.

17   I will bring dire distress upon men;
they shall walk like blind men for their sin against the
LORD.

Their blood shall be spilt like dust
and their bowels like dung;

18   neither their silver nor their gold
shall avail to save them.

On the day of the LORD's wrath, by the fire of his
jealousy
the whole land shall be consumed;
for he will make an end, a swift end,
of all who live in the land.

✻ The passage begins with an announcement like verse 7.
But the style and structure of what follows is different.
Nouns dominate the sentences, painting a picture of distress
and leading to the announcement of 'a swift end' in verse 18.
Instead of the universal devastation of verses 2–6 and the
denunciation of Jerusalem in verses 7–13, judgement here
applies to 'the whole land'.

14. This verse has given translators trouble and has been
altered in the N.E.B. But new light has come from an
Egyptian papyrus. Then we may render the text:

'The great day of the LORD is near.
The great Soldier himself is near.
The noise of the day of the LORD is overpowering
shouting: See the Warrior!'

The Day is one of battle and the LORD's appearance on the field will decide the outcome (cp. Isa. 42: 13).

15. This is some of the best poetry in the Old Testament. Like an old battle-song it pictures the effect of the LORD's going into battle. *wrath* pictures the LORD's response to enmity and rebellion. *a day of wrath* is the moment when he finally acts against his opposition. It is a part of the final judgement in the prophetic descriptions and is also found in Romans and Revelation.

17. A new speech by the LORD begins here. *men* is mankind. The prophecy returns to the theme of universal judgement of verse 3. *their sin* is *against the LORD*, not the breaking of the law, but treason against a rightful ruler. *dust* may also mean 'mud', a better comparison for 'blood'. The word rendered *bowels* may also mean 'their sap of life', a better parallel to 'their blood' in the previous line. Thus the lines could read:

> 'Their blood shall be spilt like mud
> and their sap of life like dung.'

18. *their silver nor their gold* probably refers to idols (cp. Isa. 2: 20; Hos. 2: 8). *an end...by the fire:* cp. Nahum 1: 8. *the land:* this judgement has moved from the city back to the wider territory of verse 4, but it is spoken in terms of the universal destruction heard in verses 2–3. ✳

A CALL TO SEEK MERCY

Gather together, you unruly nation, gather together, **2**
before you are sent far away and vanish[a] like chaff,   2
before the burning anger of the LORD comes upon you,
before the day of the LORD's anger comes upon you.
    Seek the LORD,   3
all in the land who live humbly by his laws,
seek righteousness, seek a humble heart;

[a] you are...vanish: *prob. rdg.; Heb. obscure.*

> it may be that you will find shelter
> in the day of the LORD's anger.

4 For Gaza shall be deserted,
> Ashkelon left desolate,
> the people of Ashdod shall be driven out[a] at noonday
> and Ekron uprooted.

✻ The terrible day has been announced, but it has not actually come. Before it does come the prophet, hoping to avoid the predicted destruction, calls for the people to turn to the LORD (cp. Amos 5: 6, 14). The text is full of possible double meanings and implied suggestions.

1. *Gather together:* the original words and their grammatical forms are unusual. They may mean to gather stubble or wood for a fire. This is in line with the mention of fire in 1: 18 and of 'chaff' and 'burning' that follow.

you unruly nation is addressed to the inhabitants of Jerusalem. The people of God are usually called a 'people' and the word 'nation' is used mainly for the heathen so that it became a synonym for 'heathen'. But here, Jerusalem is deliberately classed with the foreign nations, as it will be again in 3: 1–7. It had become so foreign in its ways that it seemed to belong more to them than to God.

But the word rendered 'gather together' may also mean 'enter hard labour'; this would fit the literal sense of the obscure words which open verse 2 and which seem to refer to 'child-birth'.

unruly translates words which mean 'who cared for nothing'. This points back to 1: 12 where the LORD found people saying, 'The LORD will do nothing, good or bad.' The idea is continued in the following lines:

> 'Gather yourselves together, gather,
> you nations that cared for nothing,

[a] the people...out: *or* Ashdod shall be made an example.

> before the womb gives birth like chaff
>   when the day has passed by;
> before "nothing" will come upon you:
>   the burning anger of the LORD;
> before "nothing" will come upon you;
>   the day of the LORD's anger.'

* The passage uses the figure of the expectant mother who refuses to take seriously the coming birth. This is the way the people of Jerusalem feel about this crucial situation which is 'pregnant' with the ominous signs of the LORD's coming judgement. Yet the people 'care for nothing'. They do not believe that the LORD is going to do anything. This negligence will lead to a false labour or a still-birth. So the people are called to 'get themselves together' *before* the critical time.

The prophet may deliberately have given a vague double picture of that awful day, which may remind one simultaneously of a raging fire or of birth-pangs (cp. Isa. 33: 11; 59: 4ff.).

3. How should they respond to this announcement? The prophet answers: *Seek the LORD* (cp. Amos 5: 6). Five lines in Hebrew begin with the letter 'b': three times with the word for 'before' and twice with the word for 'seek'. These two words dominate the appeal: 'before the day, Seek the LORD'. The proper response to the announcement of doom is not to flee. Other prophets have shown that this is impossible. It is to turn to God, to seek him out in the ways he has revealed.

all in the land: the call is for everyone in Judah. *humbly* is a noun in the Hebrew which has been translated 'the meek' or 'the poor'. But it means something more specific than that. It has the idea of being dependent. The poor are economically dependent and must commit themselves to someone for security and provision. The reference here is to those who are dependent on the LORD and who have committed themselves to him. Habakkuk, in 2: 4, was speaking of the same kind of people who in their 'faithful' way of life would 'live' and who deserved to be called the 'righteous'. *who live...by his laws* is literally, 'who do his justice'. They are those whose actions exemplify the LORD's justice. *seek righteousness* (cp. Amos 5: 14, 24): by citing the words 'justice' and 'righteousness' Zephaniah has touched on the themes of Amos and Isaiah in the century before. *seek a humble heart:* the prophet calls them to seek the state of being dependent on, and committed to, the LORD. The Beatitudes speak of 'those of a gentle spirit' who 'shall have the earth for their possession' (Matt. 5: 5). The Bible not infrequently contends that the rich are generally proud and self-sufficient, but that the 'poor' are meek, dependent and committed; they have faith.

it may be means 'perhaps'. There is no promise. But it is a chance worth taking since no other option offers a possibility of survival.

4. This verse is a bridge between the call to seek mercy and the oracles against foreign nations. *For* connects the verse to the preceding exhortations as a support for their pleas. The reason for urgency is that God's war against his enemies is about to begin. *at noonday* is the time for a noon nap. Nothing stirs in an eastern village in the hot period over noon. An attack at that time would find everyone asleep. *Gaza, Ashkelon, Ashdod* and *Ekron* were Philistine cities. The war begins with an attack on them. Goliath, from Gath, another Philistine city, is the Old Testament's strongest illustration of arrogance and blasphemy against God (1 Sam. 17).

This is the first spark of a flame that will engulf the land; and then the world will feel the heat of divine judgement (cp. 1: 18; 3: 8). This is the reason for the urgent appeals for people to 'Seek the LORD' before it is too late. ✳

ORACLES AGAINST THE NATIONS

✵ Judgement on the nations was a regular part of the religious ceremonies of 'the great day of the LORD'. (See p. 5: 'The form and role of foreign prophecy'.) These oracles pick up the references to the Philistine cities and begin the cycle of threats with them. ✵

AGAINST THE PHILISTINE CITIES

Listen, you who live by the coast, you Kerethite settlers.   5
   The word of the LORD is spoken against you;
   I will subdue you,*a* land of the Philistines,
   I will lay you waste and leave you without inhabitants,
and*b* you, Kereth, shall be all shepherds' huts*c* and   6
     sheepfolds;
and the coastland shall belong to the survivors of Judah.   7
   They shall pasture their flocks by the sea*d*
   and lie down at evening in the houses of Ashkelon,
   for the LORD their God will turn to them
     and restore their fortunes.

✵ 5. *Listen* is literally 'woe'. This word and the type of oracle it introduces was probably adopted from funeral laments. When the prophets spoke them, they seemed more like curses. Here the lament is spoken against people who are called by name. Usually it is followed only by descriptions of certain actions or attitudes. This is the beginning of God's accusation or indictment. *who live by the coast:* the inhabitants of cities belonging to the coastal league. *the coast* translates an interesting phrase. It is literally, 'a district of the sea'. 'district'

[a] I...you: *prob. rdg.; Heb.* Canaan.
[b] *So Sept.; Heb. adds* the region of the sea.
[c] you...huts: *Heb. has these words in a different order.*
[d] by the sea: *prob. rdg.; Heb.* upon them.

is a word meaning 'what is bound together'. Ugaritic parallels suggest that it may also mean 'flock'. The same word occurs in verses 6 and 7 where it tends toward the second meaning. Multiple meanings provided colour to the words as they were originally spoken. *Kerethite settlers* is literally, 'nation of Cretans'. As a 'nation' they are addressed in the first of these oracles of doom. The Philistines were generally known as soldier-colonists from Crete who had settled this coastal area of Palestine late in the twelfth century B.C. David's royal bodyguard was called 'the Kerethites and Pelethites' (cp. 2 Sam. 8: 18). *I will subdue you:* the Hebrew text (cp. footnote) has 'Canaan, *land of the Philistines*'; this would be an unusual identification of the areas. The N.E.B. adopts a very simple emendation.

6. 'the region of the sea' (footnote) may be repeated accidentally from verse 5, but if *Kereth* is understood as a noun meaning 'pastures' and the word rendered *huts* is taken in a possible meaning 'meadows' we could get: 'and the region of the sea will become meadows, pastures for shepherds, and sheepfolds'. *sheepfolds* were the simple stone enclosures in which sheep could be kept overnight. The highly developed culture of walled towns which had characterized these people for more than four centuries would disappear.

7. *the coastland* is the same word as that commented on in verse 5, meaning 'district' of the Philistine cities. But here the meaning 'flock' may be emphasized as the following lines show. *shall belong:* this area was not conquered by Joshua. With the possible exception of Solomon's reign, it had never been under Israelite or Judaean rule. But it certainly belonged to the larger area promised to Abraham, to Moses, and to David. *survivors* is a word used regularly for persons still alive after the great judgement day. *pasture their flocks* picks up the descriptions from verse 6. *by the sea:* or 'upon them' (cp. footnote); the reference is to the district formerly inhabited by Philistines. *Ashkelon* was one of their cities, lying on the coast.

for can also be read as 'when'. *will turn to them* misses the clear meaning 'he will punish them'. *their* must refer to the 'survivors of Judah'. The idiom translated *restore their fortunes* pictures a total rehabilitation for Judah after the catastrophe. The line would then read: 'when the LORD their God punishes them he shall restore their fortunes'. ✶

AGAINST MOAB AND AMMON

I have heard the insults of Moab, the taunts of Ammon, 8
  how they have insulted my people
    and encroached on their*ᵃ* frontiers.
  Therefore, by my life, 9
says the LORD of Hosts, the God of Israel,
Moab shall be like Sodom,
  Ammon like Gomorrah,
a pile of weeds, a rotting heap of saltwort,
  waste land for evermore.
The survivors of my people shall plunder them,
the remnant of my nation shall possess their land.

✶ 8. *Moab* and *Ammon* were two small countries east of the River Jordan. The earliest battles in the conquest of Canaan were against these peoples (Num. 21–4). Israelite traditions suggested that they were the descendants of the incestuous union of Lot and his daughters (Gen. 19: 30–8). But the accusations against them here have contemporary relevance. They have *insulted* God's *people* and through them God himself. They have *encroached* (literally 'made themselves great') on their frontiers. This may reflect military pressure when Judah was weak.

9. *by my life* introduces an oath. God swears that their destruction will make them like *Sodom* and *Gomorrah* (Gen. 19: 24–5); Isa. 1: 9 uses the same comparison of Jerusalem.

[*a*] *Or, with Sept.,* my.

the LORD of Hosts: the title evokes God as he rides to battle
with his symbol the Ark of the Covenant (cp. 1 Sam. 4: 3).
God of Israel is a reminder that his relation to his own people
determines his relation to others. *waste land:* the result will be
even more devastating than the judgement on the Philistines.

survivors: cp. comment on verse 7. *my people:* the term is
broader than 'Judah' in verse 7; neither is used in a narrow
nationalistic sense, but both refer to those who through faith
and covenant belong to God. *shall plunder them:* this idea
occurs regularly in scenes of God's judgements. The Israelites
took spoils in leaving Egypt (Exod. 3: 22; 12: 36). The Servant
of the LORD is said to share spoils with the great in his triumph
(Isa. 53: 12). The same words are used in the New Testament
to describe Christ's victory (e.g. Matt. 12: 29). It means that
God's people will participate in the fruits of his victory. *my
nation* refers to Judah. *possess their land* is literally, 'disinherit
them'. Their territory belongs to the larger area which God
had promised to the children of Abraham and to David's
kingdom as an 'inheritance'. The word became a technical
term for the fulfilment of God's promise. *

RETRIBUTION FOR PRIDE

10 This will be retribution for their pride, because they
have insulted the people of the LORD of Hosts and en-
11 croached upon their rights. The LORD will appear against
them with all his terrors; for he will reduce to beggary
all the gods of the earth, and all the coasts and islands of
the nations will worship him, every man in his own home.

* 10. At this point, halfway through the denunciation of
the nations, two explanatory verses in prose appear. *This:* the
word may also have the meaning of 'shame' here as has been
suggested for Job 17: 8; Mal. 2: 13 (N.E.B. 'here') and Deut.

32: 6. This would make the line read: 'Shame to them because of their pride.' Then it picks up words from the previous accusation, *insulted* and *encroached*. Because their attitudes and acts were against *the people of the LORD of Hosts*, they are judged to be against his own person and his territory.

11. *will appear...with all his terrors* translates a single word which means 'fearful' or 'to be feared'. Some interpreters think it was originally a similar word meaning 'he will appear'. The translation has used both meanings. The LORD is fearful and to be feared. The worship in Jerusalem stressed this aspect of his holiness. It is particularly appropriate when he confronts heathen gods. The simplest translation is: 'The LORD is fearful against them.' *reduce to beggary* means he will rule over them totally. *gods of the earth* are the Canaanite gods 'of the land' who were worshipped in Moab and Ammon. The subduing of the gods will lead to all men worshipping the LORD. The N.E.B. changes subjects here, but the Hebrew may be rendered: 'and they (the gods) shall bow down to him, each from his own place (from his own temple), all the demons of the nations'. The word translated *coasts and islands* may here have another meaning: 'jackals' (as in Isa. 13: 22 and elsewhere). Then 'jackals' parallels 'the gods of the earth'. So they may best be the ghosts or demons that were thought to inhabit old ruins. A major part of God's victory is over all gods and demons (cp. Ps. 82). Jesus' mastery of the demons was understood as a sign that 'the kingdom of God has already come' (Matt. 12: 28). This does not necessarily authenticate the existence of other gods. It does present the LORD's claim to sole reign and power in a language that was universally understood. *

AGAINST CUSH AND NINEVEH

12   You Cushites also shall be killed
        by the sword of the LORD.[a]

13   So let him stretch out his hand over the north
        and destroy Assyria,
    make Nineveh desolate,
        arid as the wilderness.

14   Flocks shall couch there,
        and all the beasts of the wild.
  Horned owl and ruffed bustard shall roost on her
      capitals;
    the tawny owl shall hoot in the window,
        and the bustard stand in the porch.[b]

15   This is the city that exulted in fancied security,
    saying to herself, 'I am, and I alone.'
    And what is she now? A waste, a haunt for wild beasts,
    at which every passer-by shall hiss and shake his fist.

✻ 12. This brief announcement of doom to the Cushites is
so terse that it is difficult to translate. Literally it is: 'Already
you Cushites were pierced by his sword.' There is no verb
to determine what English tense should be used. *Cushites*
were Ethiopians. They were joined with Egypt through most
of their history. In 663 B.C. kings of Ethiopian ancestry ruled
Egypt. In that year the Assyrian king, Asshurbanipal, invaded
the country and destroyed Thebes (cp. note on Nahum 3: 8).
This event was recent history for Zephaniah and makes an
appropriate introduction to the oracle against Assyria. In this
case the past tense would be better.

  13. *stretch out his hand:* the phrase applies to judgement as

[a] the sword of the LORD: *prob. rdg.;* Heb. my sword.
[b] *Prob. rdg.;* Heb. *adds an unintelligible phrase.*

well as to battle. The Philistine districts were south-west of Jerusalem. Moab and Ammon lay east of the city. Ethiopia was south. Now the judgement turns to the *north*, the most feared direction (cp. e.g. Jer. 1: 15; cp. note on Joel 2: 20). *Assyria* combined in its reality and reputation the fearful characteristics of every invader (cp. the commentary on Nahum). *Nineveh* was her main city (cp. the section of this volume on Nahum and Jonah), and is to suffer the doom spoken over other nations: she will revert to an uninhabited wilderness. God's judgement releases the destructive forces within a civilization to erode its order and culture until it collapses. Nineveh was destroyed in 612 B.C. only about two decades after this was spoken.

14. *Flocks*: the theme of verses 7 and 9 reappears. *all the beasts of the wild*: the return to primeval conditions has the *owl* and the *bustard* roosting on what were once the elaborate capitals of buildings of state.

15. *This* refers to the ruined city. *is* may better be the future, 'will be', and *exulted* a present, 'exults'. The prophet has laid bare the future which strips away the disguise of glory to reveal only cheap tinsel and a fraudulent façade. '*I am, and I alone*': this same phrase is applied to Babylon's arrogance about a century later by the Second Isaiah (Isa. 47: 8, 10). *I alone* may refer to 'the extremity of power'. The whole arrogant claim means, 'I and all the power there is'. *And what is she now?* a translation in the future tense would be better: 'what shall she be?' *at which* introduces a common prophetic description of the horror and amazement which the ruins will evoke from those who pass by (cp. the similar judgement on Jerusalem and the temple in 1 Kings 9: 8). ✳

AGAINST JERUSALEM, THE TYRANT CITY

3   Shame on the tyrant city, filthy and foul!

2   No warning voice did she heed, she took no rebuke to heart,
    she did not trust in the LORD or come near to her God.

3   Her officers were lions roaring in her midst,
     her rulers wolves of the plain[a]
     that did not wait[b] till morning,

4   her prophets were reckless, no true prophets.
     Her priests profaned the sanctuary
      and did violence to the law.

5   But the LORD in her midst is just;
      he does no wrong;
    morning by morning he gives judgement,
     without fail at daybreak.[c]

✻ From the greatest world power of that day the cycle of judgement turns to Zion, the LORD's own dwelling. It is not called by name, but there can be no doubt of the identification. The prophet places it in the group of nations to be judged, just as Amos put Judah and Israel at the end of his list (cp. Amos 2: 4ff.).

1. *Shame* is the word often translated 'Woe'. *tyrant* refers to violence and oppression. Almost a century earlier Isaiah used similar words about Jerusalem (Isa. 1: 21–3).

2. *warning voice* seems to be a direct reference to the prophecies of Isaiah. There could be no greater sin than failure to heed God's warnings. *trust* is an inner attitude or conviction. *come near* is the act of worship which gives the inner attitude shape. Jerusalem had done neither. In Isaiah's

[a] *Or* evening.
[b] *Or* carry off.
[c] *Prob. rdg.; Heb. adds* but the wrongdoer knows no shame.

time its people had performed acts of worship which did not conform to their convictions. Zephaniah accuses them of doing neither. It may be that their worship was offered to alien deities. The emphases in the verse are on *the LORD* and *her God*. Because they lacked any strong relation to him, the moral chaos, unchecked oppressions, and false religion of a heathen city were at home there. The entire picture is that of a present situation and should be translated in the present tense.

3. *Her officers* begins the list of ruthless men of power. *lions roaring* pictures men of rapacious greed. *in her midst* is parallel to the description of the LORD's presence in verse 5. *rulers* are 'judges'. *wolves* describe the preying habits of those whose duty it is to bring about justice. *of the plain* has changed the Hebrew 'of the evening'. The original is set opposite *till morning* and makes good sense. But the phrase should be understood as 'since morning'. The lines then read:

> 'her judges are wolves at evening
>   who have had nothing on which to gnaw since morning.'

These wolves have nocturnal hunting habits and begin their hunt in the evening when they are ravenous from an entire day without food. They may be contrasted to the wolf in Gen. 49: 27 who had killed so much in the night that he could feast on it through the following day.

4. *her prophets:* religious leaders are also implicated. *reckless* here means 'boastful'. *no true prophets* is literally 'men of faithless acts'. The people had no confidence in these men who supposedly spoke for God. Jeremiah found them equally untrustworthy some decades later (Jer. 8: 10). *Her priests:* in Israel priests had two responsibilities. One was to deal with holy things like the sanctuary, the sacrifice, and holy days. The other required them to instruct people in keeping the law of God. *profaned the sanctuary* relates to the first duty, but 'sanctuary' should probably be understood in a broader sense as 'that which is holy'. Ezek. 22: 26 apparently quotes this

passage and adds: 'They make no distinction between sacred and common, and lead men to see no difference between clean and unclean.' *did violence to* has the sense of 'break' or 'distort' *the law*.

5. As though to show that not all of Jerusalem is corrupt, the prophet speaks of God. Four lines have begun with officers, rulers, prophets, and priests. The fifth begins with *the LORD*. Human leaders may all be wrong, but he *is just*. He is right. And he, like the leaders, is *in her midst*. He has not abandoned the city. And *he does no wrong*.

morning was the usual time when court was in session and justice meted out. *he gives judgement:* in Hebrew, 'his judgement'. *without fail at daybreak* is literally, 'at the light which does not fail'. 'Light' refers to the sun. 'which does not fail' has a double reference to the sunrise (cp. Isa. 40: 26) and to the LORD's justice.

The N.E.B. has omitted a line (cp. footnote). The usual translation seems to mean that 'the wrong-doer' has 'no shame' or does not recognize that what he has done is worthy of shame. But the word 'shame' may be a derisive term for Baal (cp. e.g. Hos. 9: 10) meaning 'shameful god' or 'god of shame'. If so, these lines pose 'the LORD, the righteous, who never does wrong', over against Baal, 'the god of shame who does not even recognize the wrong-doer'. The LORD 'searches Jerusalem' with the light of his justice. Baal is blind to all this and unable to establish justice. Ps. 82: 5 declares that heathen gods are total failures in establishing justice. ✻

THE LORD'S ACCUSATION

6   I have wiped out the proud;[a]
       their battlements are laid in ruin.
    I have made their streets a desert where no one passes.

[a] *So Sept.; Heb.* nations.

Their cities are laid waste, deserted, unpeopled.
In the hope that she would remember[a] all my instruc- 7
tions,
I said, 'Do but fear me
and take my rebuke to heart';
but they were up betimes and went about their evil
deeds.

Wait for me, therefore, says the LORD, 8
wait for the day when I stand up to accuse you;
for mine it is to gather nations
and assemble kingdoms,
to pour out on them my indignation,
all the heat of my anger;
the whole earth shall be consumed by the fire of my
jealousy.

✲ The LORD sums up the threats against the nations including
Jerusalem.

6. *proud:* the original word (cp. footnote) 'nations' should
be kept. It is the key word in the section. The fall of great
empires was God's doing and was a preview of the great
judgement day.

7. *I said* has the sense, 'I thought'. It pictures God's wish
which, unfortunately, did not come true. '*Do but fear me*':
this is a conditional clause which requires the part left out
(cp. footnote) to complete its sense:

'I said, "If only you would fear me
and take my rebuke to heart,
Your dwelling would not be destroyed
according to all that I have planned against you."'

The entire verse states God's wish, which is contrary to fact.
Judah chose the opposite course.

[a] she would remember: *prob. rdg., cp. Sept.; Heb.* her dwelling-place
would not be cut off.

8. *Wait for me* could be a call for the kind of faithful patience pictured in Hab. 2: 4. But here it is a command from the king and judge. *when I stand up to accuse you:* the translation has the right idea, but a literal rendering: 'when I rise from my throne', emphasizes more the sovereign status of the accusing judge. *mine* means 'my judgement' or 'my decision'. The scene returns to the universal judgement with which the book began (cp. also Joel 3: 9–15). ✵

GOD'S ULTIMATE GOAL

9   I will give all peoples once again pure lips,
      that they may invoke the LORD by name
      and serve him with one consent.

10   From beyond the rivers of Cush
      my suppliants of the Dispersion shall bring me tribute.

✵ The change is sudden. The festival pattern expected the terrible judgement scenes to be necessary preludes to God's merciful acts of salvation. The prophets are working within that pattern.

9. The verse in Hebrew begins with exclamatory particles that have not been translated: 'Yes! Then...' These set off the change of mood in the new verses. *I will give* means 'transform' or 'change'. *all peoples* is literally, 'unto the peoples'. *pure lips* is singular: 'a purged lip'. Isaiah was conscious of his own and his people's sin in terms of 'unclean lips' (Isa. 6: 5). The passage may also reflect the curse that has been humanity's burden since God's judgement on the builders of the Tower of Babel (Gen. 11: 1–9). There the issue was 'to make a name for ourselves'. God noted that they were of one 'lip' or language and brought judgement by confusing their speech. God's new act beyond the judgement will reverse this. The peoples will be given a purged language which will no longer be confused. With it they *may*

178

invoke the LORD by name rather than making a name for
themselves. They will *serve* or worship the LORD instead of
being scattered over the face of the earth. *with one consent* is
an idiom, literally 'with one shoulder', like our 'shoulder to
shoulder'. 'A pure lip' and 'one shoulder' are parallel in the
poem just as the one speech and co-operative labour went
together in building the Tower of Babel.

10. *From beyond the rivers of Cush* are the dimly recognized
limits of civilization as the prophet knew them. *my suppliants
of the Dispersion:* this expression often means the scattered
people of Israel, but the parallels to Gen. 11 suggest that the
scattered and confused peoples of the world are intended here.
shall bring me tribute: pilgrims from the extremes of civilization
will approach Jerusalem to recognize the LORD as king over
all. The kingdom of God on earth will have become a
reality. *

A remnant preserved

* Two speeches of the LORD are interspersed with joyful
cries by the prophet. The purge of God's judgement will produce a people of Zion capable of worship in purity and joy. *

On that day, Jerusalem,   11
    you shall not be put to shame for all your deeds
        by which you have rebelled against me;
    for then I will rid you
        of your proud and arrogant citizens,
    and never again shall you flaunt your pride
        on my holy hill.
    But I will leave in you a people   12
        afflicted and poor.

13   The survivors in Israel shall find refuge in the name of
the LORD;
> they shall no longer do wrong or speak lies,
> no words of deceit shall pass their lips;
> for they shall feed and lie down
> with no one to terrify them.

✻ 11. *that day* is the one in verse 8. *you* is properly understood
to be Jerusalem although this is not in the Hebrew. It is clear
from *my holy hill* at the end of the verse. Jerusalem's guilt is
plain for all to see. *for then* are the same words which opened
verse 9 but which were not translated there. But God will act
to purify her: *I will rid you. proud and arrogant:* these are two
words of exultation and wild haughtiness belonging to a
festival. They can turn serious religious gatherings into
carnivals. They explain *rebelled against me* of the previous line.
flaunt your pride means show your arrogance. *my holy hill* is
the temple area on Zion. This oracle shows the same zeal that
the temple (cp. Ps. 69: 9) be respected and kept holy that
Jesus showed when he whipped the vendors out of its courts
(e.g. Matt. 21: 12–13).

12. *I will leave in you* is literally, 'I will cause to survive
in your midst.' *a people:* from earliest times God wanted 'a
people' that he could call his own. Through the cataclysmic
events of 'that day' he will create the people he has wanted.
In contrast to the proud and haughty revellers, these will be
the afflicted who have committed themselves to the LORD
and are dependent on his mercy (cp. comment on 2: 3). The
poor are the helpless, insignificant persons who were often
of the oppressed classes. Paul wrote to the Christian church
in Corinth reminding them of these characteristics of the
true people of God (1 Cor. 1: 26–8).

13. *find refuge* is joined directly to the *people* of verse 12.
Since they are dependent and helpless, they fall back on the
only refuge that is adequate for 'that day'. These *survivors*

are all that remain of God's people. They will *no longer* do
the sins of the past. *do wrong* probably refers to idol worship.
speak lies may also refer to the ritual sayings of heathen
worship (cp. 1 : 5). With *lips* made pure (cp. 3 : 9), there will be
no words of deceit (literally 'there shall no deceitful tongue be
found in their mouths').

for introduces a contrast and should be translated 'but'.
feed and *lie down* (cp. Ps. 23) are pictures of solemn worship
on Zion. The people receive the word of God and rest in the
assurance of his presence. This is in sharp contrast to the wild
orgies of a Baal festival (cp. the description in 1 Kings 18:
26-9). *no one to terrify them:* the quiet flock of worshippers at
rest need fear no oppressor. Also they need never again hear
the LORD's threats against wrong-doers in the land. This is the
peace to be enjoyed by those whom the LORD will save from
the holocaust. ✻

> Zion, cry out for joy;   14
> raise the shout of triumph, Israel;
> be glad, rejoice with all your heart,
> daughter of Jerusalem.
> The LORD has rid you of your adversaries,   15
> he has swept away your foes;
> the LORD is among you as king, O Israel;
> never again shall you fear disaster.

✻ The prophet accepts this good news for Jerusalem and
calls her people to rejoice and sing (Isa. 12: 4–6; Joel 2: 21–4).

14. *Zion* is the holy hill of the people of God (cp. 3: 11).
Israel is the name of God's people, those whom Moses called
from Egypt to make covenant with God. *Zion* and *Jerusalem*
are also terms used for God's people with the emphasis on
God's promises to David. These are combined in Old Testament faith and hope.

15. God's purging action is complete and there is ample

reason to rejoice. *your adversaries* is literally 'your judgements' and has been difficult to interpret. The *foe* (Hebrew singular) of God has also been the enemy of true Israelites. It may be the arch-enemy who incorporates all chaotic powers, or it may be a collective term for all the collaborators with Assyrian power and worship. Their presence in Jerusalem has made God's 'judgements' on the city necessary. God has now rid the city of its enemies and of the necessity for 'judgements'.

The triumphant shout breaks forth. Literally it is: 'King, O Israel, is the LORD in your midst.' Each element is important. *among you* or 'in your midst' is a reminder that the LORD has made his dwelling on Zion. He is now recognized as king after his successful battle against all threatening powers, nations, gods, and demons. Since he has established peace, his people need never *fear disaster* again. ✶

16   On that day this shall be the message to Jerusalem:
     Fear not, O Zion; let not your hands fall slack.

17   The LORD your God is in your midst,
       like a warrior, to keep you safe;
     he will rejoice over you and be glad;
       he will show you his love once more;[a]
     he will exult over you with a shout of joy
18a   as in days long ago.[b]

✶ 16. The prophet continues his *message to Jerusalem*. *On that day* picks up the time from verses 8 and 11. *Fear not* is the old battle-cry that announced God's participation with Israel in holy war. *let not your hands fall slack* continues the admonition for soldiers. It means, 'do not relax your discipline'.

17. Reference to God's presence is repeated, but with the reminder, *like a warrior*. *to keep you safe* translates one word

[a] he will show...more: *prob. rdg., cp. Sept.; Heb.* he will be silent in his love.
[b] as...ago: *prob. rdg.; Heb. obscure.*

meaning 'saviour'. Israel's salvation is won through God's battle against evil. She is called to be as disciplined and courageous as his army. *rejoice...and be glad:* as one would welcome a victorious soldier (1 Sam. 18: 6), or as one would send off a daughter with her family (Gen. 31: 27), or as David would have one bring sacrifice to Zion's temple (2 Chron. 23: 18). *he will show* is a difficult word (cp. footnote) which probably is related to artistic work, but may also refer to composing a song. *his love* is literally, 'by his love' or 'in his love'. The line may read, 'He will sing in his love.'

18*a*. *as in days long ago* has been attached to verse 17, but in the Hebrew it is the beginning of the next sentence. An alternative rendering is suggested below. ✲

> I will take your cries of woe*a* away from you;   18*b*
> and you shall no longer endure reproach for her.
> When that time comes, see,   19
> I will deal with all your oppressors.
> I will rescue the lost and gather the dispersed;
> I will win my people praise and renown
>   in all the world where once they were despised.
> When the time comes for me to gather you,*b*   20
>   I will bring you home.
> I will win you renown and praise
>   among all the peoples of the earth,
>   when I bring back your prosperity; and you shall
>   see it.
>   It is the LORD who speaks.

[*a*] cries of woe: *prob. rdg.; Heb. obscure.*
[*b*] When... you: *prob. rdg.; Heb.* and in the time, my gathering you.

✶ Verse 18 is difficult to translate. The N.E.B. has attempted extensive changes, giving a general picture of the people's reversal of fortune. A fairly literal translation would read:

'Those of the assembly who have turned away from me
I have gathered out from among you.
They were those who were heaping disgrace upon her.'

The line refers to the apostates of 1: 5–6. 'the assembly' is the festival gathering on Zion. 'I have gathered' is what God has already done. The next verses change the tense to acts in the future. 'gathered' has a negative sense like 'weeded out' (cp. 1: 2f.). 'heaping disgrace': by acts of apostasy toward idols (cp. 1: 2–6). *her* refers to the city as a place, while the rescued inhabitants of the city are addressed.

19. To *deal with all your oppressors* is the negative side of judgement by which the positive results are achieved. *the lost* is literally, 'the lame'. *the dispersed* is the one who has strayed. The figure of the shepherd dominates God's word about his people. The entire verse speaks of the exiled peoples. *oppressors* are the Assyrians. The 'lame' and the *dispersed* are the exiles from Samaria and others who have been taken away through the years of Assyrian dominance. *When that time comes* looks forward to the time when the yoke will be totally broken.

A second phase of God's promised rehabilitation deals with their reputation which had been badly damaged during the previous century. *I will win* is literally, 'I will establish'. *my people* correctly interprets the simple 'them' of the original. *praise and renown* translates 'for a praise and for a name'. Whether the praise will be for God or for the people is unclear. Perhaps it does not matter. As the rehabilitation of the Israelites takes place, people *in all the world* who had despised both them and their God would change their minds.

20. *bring you home* catches the emotional tone. For God *to gather* Israel's dispersed people can only mean to bring them home to Zion. What God had said to Zion's assembly he now addresses to the scattered peoples themselves. They will be a

subject of *renown and praise among all the peoples of the earth* when God, acting from Zion, transforms all history to *bring back your prosperity*. Their grief will change to allow them to join the songs of praise and triumph of Zion's assembled congregation (cp. 3: 14). They will *see* the victory and participate in the festival that celebrates God's triumph. God's own word confirms this. ✶

A NOTE ON FURTHER READING

Readers requiring fuller and more detailed treatment of these books may consult commentaries like that by W. A. Maier on Nahum (Concordia, 1959) or by the editor on Obadiah (Eerdmans, 1969). The short commentary by J. H. Eaton (S.C.M. Torch series, 1961) is very useful, as are those in the 'New Peake's Commentary' (Nelson, 1962) and the *Jerome Biblical Commentary* (Prentice-Hall, 1968).

For background material readers are referred to articles in Bible dictionaries and to the relevant volumes of the *New Clarendon Bible* (Oxford University Press): E. W. Heaton, *The Hebrew Kingdoms* (1968) and Peter R. Ackroyd, *Israel under Babylon and Persia* (1970).

General treatments of prophecy with sections on these books include E. W. Heaton's *The Old Testament Prophets* (Penguin Books, 1958) and Gerhard von Rad's *The Message of the Prophets* (S.C.M. 1968).

INDEX